Suicide MUKT BHARAT

CHUPPI TODO, ZINDAGI CHUNO

ARCHANA SINHA BHANDARI (PH.D)

BlueRoseONE.com
Stories Matter
NewDelhi • London

BLUEROSE PUBLISHERS
India | U.K.

BlueRose ONE
Stories Matter
New Delhi • London

For permissions, requests or inquiries regarding this publication, please contact:

BLUEROSE PUBLISHERS
www.BlueRoseONE.com
info@bluerosepublishers.com
+91 8882 898 898
+4407342408967

ISBN: **978-93-7139-261-7**

Typesetting: Sagar

First Edition: July 2025

Dedication

Every soul that left this world quietly carried pain too heavy to put into words. Even when the world was too loud to hear the pain, they mattered. Their lives, their stories and their existence, all of it mattered.

This book is for them and for those still breathing through the weight of it all.

To the survivors, your courage is not quiet,

It's a roar that tells the world: "I chose life".

May your strength light the path for others still searching for hope.

In Gratitude

I am deeply grateful to every voice silent or spoken that has shaped this journey.

To the survivors who found the courage to share their pain and to the families who allowed me into their grief, your strength and honesty gave this book its purpose.

To my mentors and supporters who stood beside me with faith and encouragement. Thank you for guiding this mission when the path felt uncertain.

And to the divine presence that walked with me through the darkest questions, I offer my deepest gratitude.

This book is a tribute to all of you. It carries your stories and your hope. .

Acknowledgment

This book is not just ink on paper.

It is a piece of my soul stitched together with tears, pain, purpose and prayer.

This book was born not from research alone, but from the raw cries I heard, the silences I felt, including my own.

To my kids, all my family members your innocent smiles kept me breathing even on the days I felt broken inside. You are the reason I choose life again and again.

To the nurses, caregivers and kind strangers who show up without applause your small acts of compassion saved lives that no one will ever know about. I see you. I honor you.

To the readers of this book, thank you for walking through these doors of pain and truth with me. If even one soul chooses life because of these words, this journey will have been worth everything.

To God, my eternal universe, thank you for choosing me for this purpose. For holding my hand when I had no one to talk to. For turning my tears into a mission that now breathes in every page of this book.

With folded hands and a heart full of love,

Archana Sinha Bhandari

Founder, Suicide Mukt Bharat Movement

Vision of the Book: Suicide Mukt Bharat

"A nation where no life is lost to hopelessness."

The vision of Suicide Mukt Bharat is bold yet deeply necessary to awaken a collective national consciousness where mental health is prioritized, empathy is normalized, every individual feels seen/heard and supported.

This book was born not just out of statistics, but out of sorrow;- sorrow for every farmer who felt unheard, every student who felt like a failure, every youth trapped in addiction, every soul betrayed in love. These aren't just stories of individuals they are echoes of a larger societal silence.

<u>Our vision is:</u>

- To break the stigma around suicide and mental illness in India.
- To give voice to the voiceless victims, survivors, families and those on the edge.
- To educate, equip and empower citizens with the tools to recognize early signs of suicidal tendencies.
- To urge for systemic change in schools, workplaces, villages and urban homes.
- To shift India's mindset from "Why did they do it?" to "How can
- we prevent it together?"

We envision a Bharat where:

- Asking for help is not shameful.
- Mental health is not a luxury.
- Each citizen becomes a gatekeeper of hope for someone else.

This book was not planned...it was felt.

There wasn't a single moment that led me to write it, but many moments that refused to let me stay silent. The late-night phone calls. The trembling hands in counselling sessions. The families are left with questions that may never have answers. I carried those moments home with me and eventually they found their way to these pages.

Writing about suicide is not easy. It means sitting with stories that don't have happy endings. It means confronting systems that failed and feelings that were buried. There were days I stepped away from writing not because I didn't care, but because I cared too much. I wanted to get it right. I still do.

This book is not written as an expert looking down, but as a human sitting beside. It's for every person who has felt overwhelmed and for every person who has ever wondered how to help someone else.

Let us, together, dream and strive for a **Suicide Mukt Bharat** not as a slogan, but as a shared reality.

The Unseen Epidemic: Understanding Suicide

Across India, lives are being lost not just to mental illness, but to isolation and injustice. Behind every suicide is a deeper wound: the boy mocked for expressing emotion, the girl silenced after abuse, the LGBTQ+ youth rejected by their own family, the father drowning in debt with no way out.

Some students break under the pressure of marks, employees who are pushed to the edge by toxic work environments, a girl died; "not from rape but from what the world said after" and young people bullied until their will to live disappears. These are not isolated cases. They are quietly becoming normal and that is what disturbs me the most.

This book matters because it dares to confront what we often avoid. It doesn't just talk about suicide as a mental health issue. It reveals the social, emotional and systemic pressures that drive people toward the unthinkable:

- Loan burden and financial distress
- Bullying and humiliation
- Sexual abuse and silence
- Organizational pressure and workplace harassment
- Academic failure and exam pressure
- Gender discrimination against men
- Rejection of LGBTQ+ identities

These are not just "issues." They are everyday realities for millions. And unless we name them, understand them and address them- the cycle will continue.

This book is not just a guide. It is a mirror and a bridge; a mirror to see ourselves clearly and a bridge to reach those who feel alone or afraid to speak for themselves.

Because if even one person feels understood and heard after reading these pages- then this book has already begun to matter.

The Silent Storm Within

Suicide is not just the end of a life it is the end of a long, often invisible, inner war. It's the final cry of a heart that held on for too long, silently screaming for relief, not attention. In a country as emotionally vibrant as India-where community, spirituality and family bonds are valued. The rising tide of suicide paints a paradox we can no longer ignore. Every day, nearly 450 Indians die by suicide. That's one every three minutes. But these aren't just numbers.

They are:

- A mother who couldn't escape domestic cruelty.
- A student who cracked under the weight of expectations.
- A man who wore a smile but carried a storm inside.
- A farmer who watered fields others would harvest but couldn't
- save himself.

They leave behind unanswered questions, broken families and a society that often prefers silence over introspection.

Why Is Suicide Increasing?

We live in a time where we can send a message across the globe in seconds, but find it difficult to speak to the person sitting across the room.

People now choose to **text instead of talk** and vent to strangers online while going completely silent at home.

Some people sleep next to someone every night and still feel utterly alone.

When daily conversations are replaced by silence and genuine listening is replaced by judgment, emotional isolation begins to grow. And from that quiet, dangerous space... hopelessness finds its way in.

Also, India has one of the highest suicide rates globally, with thousands of individuals ending their lives each year. According to the National Crime Records Bureau (NCRB), the suicide rate in India has been rising, affecting individuals from all walks of life. And the saddest part is that these cases not only affect the individual but also leaves a lasting impact on families and communities. Families of those individuals who die by Suicide often experience immense grief, financial distress and social stigma. The loss of a loved one due to suicide can lead to increased mental health issues among surviving members.

Though I know the biggest obstacle to preventing Suicide in India is the stigma associated with mental health issues. Many people hesitate to seek help due to the fear of being judged or ostracized by society. Mental Health is often considered a "taboo" subject and individuals suffering from depression, anxiety or suicidal thoughts may find little to No support from their families or communities.

Mythological Insight

“On the battlefield of Kurukshetra, Arjuna trembled not from the fear of war but from the storm within. He was broken, ready to walk away from everything.

And Krishna... didn’t give orders.

He didn’t question him.

He stood by him. He listened. With love and with stillness.

Only then... he spoke.

Today, in the silent battles of our own kurukshetras...in a child breaking under pressure... in a woman silently crying in the kitchen,

In a man hiding his tears at work...

Be Krishna.

Listen not to reply, but to hold their pain.

Your presence could be the hand that pulls someone back from the edge.

Sometimes, that’s all it takes...

To save a Life.

Contents

Dedication i

In Gratitude ii

Acknowledgment iii

Vision of the Book: Suicide Mukt Bharat iv

The Unseen Epidemic: Understanding Suicide vi

Mythological Insight ix

Key to Door 1: This key frees you from pain at work 1

Key to Door 2: This key lightens the Loan pressure 13

Key to Door 3: This key holds a message "NEVER GIVE UP" 25

Key to Door 4: This key opens the door to "Letting Go" 39

Key to Door 5: This key shelters you from past storms 51

Key to Door 6: This key reminds: He matters beyond his duties 65

Key to Door 7: This key carries the courage they were denied 79

Key to Door 8- This key breaks false chains 91

Key to Door 9: This key honors your invisible battles 109

Key to Door 10: This key unlocks a future your soul deserved 127

STEP ONE: WARNING SIGNS 140

STEP TWO: What You Can Do – Be the Reason Someone Chooses to Stay: 141

STEP THREE: The Role of Families: Home Can Be a Lifeline or a Lonely Cage 142

STEP FOUR: The Role of Schools, Colleges & Universities: 144

STEP FIVE: The Role of Organisations: Corporates & Management Workplaces That Heal or Harm 146

STEP SIX: Healing & Recovery After a Suicide Attempt 149

Key to Door 1

THIS KEY FREES YOU FROM PAIN AT WORK

DOOR 1

When The Workplace Turns Toxic

Suicide due to workplace harassment and organisational neglect

---

The Morning They Never Returned:

They dressed up. Just like any other day. One packed her lunch. Another carried his laptop bag. They took the same train. Smiled at the security guard.

And walked into a building that slowly broke them.

What people didn't see was that behind the smile was a silence. Behind the daily meetings an exhaustion. And behind every "I'm okay" was a soul screaming: **"I'm not okay."**

But nobody heard it.

Because workplaces teach us to meet targets, not people.

We often speak of success in terms of jobs promotions, salaries and office views.

But we rarely speak of **suffocation inside cabins** of **smiles that hide tears**, of people who whisper "I'm fine" while dying inside. In the so-called professional world, **harassment doesn't always come with fists**. Sometimes it wears suits. Sits across the table. Sends emails that humiliate. Or whispers poison in group chats and team calls.

Some people don't resign from jobs they resign from life.

Real Case 1: A silent voice that never reached to HR

A bright IT engineer in Bengaluru, had dreams bigger than her pay slip. But her manager would constantly mock her, call her "too sensitive" and assign her last-minute impossible tasks.

She stayed late to prove herself. She kept silent when he "joked" about her body in meetings. She cried quietly in the washrooms until one day, she didn't show up.

They found her lifeless in her PG room, with a note that read:

"No salary is worth this silence. Please don't let another girl feel like me."

She didn't fail **her workplace did.**

Real Story 2: A Quiet Goodbye from a Senior Leader

39-year-old men, a mid-level VP in finance, seemed successful.

But behind his cabin door, he was drowning. Relentless pressure. Humiliation masked as "performance feedback." Being made the scapegoat for mistakes he never made.

In his suicide note, he wrote:

"They said 'don't be emotional.' But being emotional was the last part of me that was human. I hope in my death, someone notices what they couldn't in my life."

The Invisible Weapons at Work:

- Gaslighting by seniors- making employees doubt their own worth.
- Unrealistic deadlines- disguised as "challenges".
- Favoritism & exclusion- turning teams into cliques.
- Sexual innuendos masked as jokes.
- Lack of emotional support or safe reporting spaces.
- Labeling trauma as weakness.

Most victims of workplace harassment don't scream. They *endure*. Until they *exit* life itself.

Practical Solutions for Companies to Adapt:

- **Normalize Mental Health Days:** Make it okay to take a day off for the soul not just the body.
- **Train Leaders in Compassionate Leadership:** Teach them to lead with empathy. A good leader doesn't just manage tasks they protect people.
- **Build Support Circles at Work:** Safe spaces where employees can speak up, without being labelled as "weak."
- **Offer Anonymous Helpline Access:** Confidential mental health counselling services for all staff.
- **Start Monthly Emotional Check-ins:** "How are you feeling?" should be as important as "What's the update?"
- **Redesign Roles with Dignity:** No one should feel like a machine. Redesign roles to respect boundaries and meaning.

What Can Be Done? Human Wellness Solutions for Individuals

1. **Speak up, even if your voice shakes.**: Because silence doesn't protect you it protects the one who hurt you. Every time we stay quiet, injustice becomes stronger. Your truth matters. Your story matters. And speaking up may not be easy, but it is the first step toward reclaiming your power.
2. **Document every incident every message, email, voice note, or verbal threat.**: Even when the world chooses not to believe, your evidence will speak for you. Start a diary. Save screenshots. Record voice memos. Your pain is real and it deserves to be backed with proof.
3. **Seek therapy or join a support group.**: This is not weakness. This is wisdom. You are allowed to cry. You are allowed to be confused. Healing is not a straight line but by reaching out, you allow light into your darkness. There are people trained to help, to listen

without judgment and to walk beside you when you feel like you can't move forward alone.

4. **Connect with external bodies' labor rights organizations, women's safety cells, HR helplines, or NGOs.**: There are warriors out there whose only job is to protect people like you. Let them help. Don't carry the burden of injustice by yourself. You are not alone..... you were never meant to be.

5. **Prioritize your peace of mind over a title, a salary, or a toxic job.**: A job is replaceable. **You are not.** If a workplace makes you question your worth, suffocates your spirit, or steals your sleep it is not success. Walk away, if you must. Choose your mental health. Choose your life. There is no trophy for enduring silent suffering.

You are not just surviving you're awakening.
And every step you take toward healing is an act of courage.
You matter. You are enough. And it is never too late to begin again.

For Colleagues: Be the Reason Someone Feels Safe at Work

1. **Believe them.**: If a coworker opens up to you about abuse or harassment, don't question their truth. It takes unimaginable courage to speak up. **Your belief might be the only support they have.** Don't let them walk away feeling unheard or doubted.

2. **Don't laugh at what's called a "joke" if it sounds like cruelty.**: Because *cruelty in disguise is still cruelty.* When we laugh along with humiliating or sexist comments, even in silence, we become part of the problem. Be the one who doesn't normalize it. *Stand with the hurt, not with the hurtful.*

3. **Check in- truly, gently and often**: A simple **"How are you really doing?"** could be the only moment in someone's day when they feel seen. You don't need to fix everything but just showing that you care can pull someone back from the edge of hopelessness.

4. **Report abuse- even if you're not the victim.:** *Your silence gives the abuser a free pass.* If you witness something wrong, say something. Document it. Raise it. Support the one who's suffering. You might be the only voice they didn't know they needed.

In a world where workplaces can become battlefields of silent pain,

be the colleague who becomes someone's shelter.

Because sometimes, all it takes is one brave soul to stop a lifetime of suffering.

What Organizations Must Do: Policy Changes That Don't Just Save Jobs... But Save Lives

In workplaces across the country, behind name tags and glowing screens, people are breaking. They're smiling in meetings while silently drowning in fear, humiliation and emotional pain.

It's time for organizations to stop being just employers and start being guardians of human dignity.

1. Zero Tolerance Harassment Policy

Because protecting the victim must always come before protecting the image.

- **Every complaint should lead to immediate investigation.** No more delays. No more brushing things under the carpet.
- **Strict disciplinary action must follow within 7-15 days.** Justice that takes too long can feel like another punishment.
- **Suspend the accused pending inquiry.** Safety cannot wait for confirmation it must be immediate.

2. Mental Health Must Be Woven into Every Layer of the System

Because people shouldn't have to hit rock bottom to be offered support.

- **Provide free, confidential therapy sessions as part of employee wellness.**
  Let people talk before they break.
- **Include mental health leave.** Emotional exhaustion is as real as a fever.
- **Ensure coverage in insurance.** If physical illness is covered, why not the mind that drives everything?

3. Anonymous Grievance Redressal System

Because fear of retaliation kills truth before it can even be spoken.

- **Implement third-party portals, completely independent of the reporting chain.**
- **Provide complete whistleblower protection.** No one should lose their job for doing the right thing.

4. Psychological Safety Committees

Because one HR person isn't enough to carry the burden of emotional justice.

- Create a balanced committee with **HR personnel, a licensed mental health professional, an elected employee representative and an external ethical advisor.**
- Train this team not just to *listen*, but to *feel* and respond with humanity.

5. Emotional Exit Surveys

Behind every resignation is a story of joy, of disappointment, or of pain nobody noticed.

- Move beyond "Why did you leave?" to "How did we make you feel while you were here?"
- Use open-ended questions that invite honesty and **follow up with genuine action.**

6. Diversity & Dignity Policy

Because the right to feel safe should never depend on who you are.

- Protect employees from bias, exclusion, or discrimination based on gender, caste, religion, sexuality, physical ability, or neurodiversity.
- Offer inclusive facilities, unbiased hiring practices and language sensitivity training.

7. Post-Incident Care- Because Recovery Is a Process, Not a Policy

- After incidents of harassment, trauma, or suicide, the healing process must be **community-based and continuous.**
- Offer **counseling sessions for the team**, healing circles and open forums to grieve and understand what went wrong.
- Don't just move on. **Pause and Reflect.**

Every company policy should carry a "**Compassion Clause**" those states: "We are committed to protecting not just your productivity but your peace."

Mythological Insight:

- **Lord Rama:-** the rightful prince was unfairly exiled for 14 years, he didn't give up.

  He didn't curse the system or take revenge. He walked away from the palace not in weakness, but with inner strength.

  In the forest, he built alliances. He stayed true to his dharma.

  And,in time he returned stronger not just to reclaim a throne, but to show that dignity never dies when you walk the path of truth.

Similarly, your current workplace may feel unfair.

You may feel wronged, misunderstood, or punished. But exile is not the end. It's a transition.

- **In the *Mahabharata*:-** the court of Hastinapur watched silently as Draupadi was humiliated. Not a soldier. Not a king.

  Not even the wise, no one spoke.

That silence was the real violence. Every HR head who ignores a complaint...

Every manager who says "don't take it personally".

Every colleague who laughs when someone cries...

They're playing the same role as those silent spectators.

Let's break that cycle. Let's be Krishna, who didn't stay silent

But stepped in to protect.

Walk Out of This Door

If your hands are shaking right now....let them

Let them remind you you're still alive. That your heart still works.

That you still care.

Because this isn't just about others.

We are all someone's colleague, someone's manager, someone's human.

You now have the power to become the *reason someone stays alive* not the

reason they don't.

So, if you ever see someone withdrawing, crying alone in a restroom, staying back late in silence.

Don't ignore. Don't assume.

Be the person who notices.

Door 1 ends not in Anguish, but in choice.

Close this Door.. but walk out stronger,
with eyes open and a heart awakened.

Key to Door 2

This key lightens the Loan pressure

DEBT
DOOR
2

Dying in Debt

When Money Crushed the Soul,
This Chapter Became the Oxygen

A Note to the Reader:

If you're waking up each day with a new call from a lender, If the sound of a message alert now gives you panic, not curiosity, if you're calculating EMIs more than you calculate your dreams...

Then let this Door hold your pain and open into something **brighter**.

Real Story 1: The Golden Son Who Died in Silence

Anonymous: N, was 27. He had landed a well-paying job in Bengaluru after doing his engineering from a Tier 1 college. The pride of his parents, the "sorted one" among his friends.

But no one knew the loans he took to support his younger sibling's education and his parents' medical treatment.

No one saw him being bullied silently by digital loan apps, hounded at work, blackmailed with photos they morphed from his social media.

He smiled every day in meetings.

But one Monday morning, his roommate found him hanging from the ceiling, next to a printed screenshot of his bank statement with negative balance.

He left a short note:

"I tried my best. But I was only taught how to earn.
Not how to survive when I couldn't."

Real Story 2: The Small Business Dream That Ended at a Window Ledge

Anonymous: P, 34, ran a small boutique. Her creativity sparkled through her hands, but her books were bleeding red.

She borrowed ₹10 lakhs during the pandemic to pay employees, rent, to keep the business alive.

She mortgaged her parents' gold and took loans from private lenders.

But the sales didn't return. The calls became louder. Threatening.

One day, she told her younger brother,

"Just tell them I went away for a few days."

She jumped from the 18th floor of her apartment building and gone forever.

What We Need to Understand:

Often, it's not outsiders who break someone already crushed under the weight of debt- it's their own family.

When a child is drowning in shame, avoiding phone calls from lenders, battling sleepless nights due to loan burdens it is heartbreaking that **sometimes it is their own parents or siblings who humiliate them further.**

Instead of offering support, they add to the shame. Instead of holding them up, they push them deeper.

But this is where everything must change.

If your son, daughter, brother, or sister is struggling, **be the first one to stand.**

If debt collectors are calling and shaming your loved one.....don't become another voice that breaks them. Be the voice that **builds them.**

If you can support them financially....even a little, **do it.**

If you can't, **then offer the strength of your words.** Say:

*"**You're not alone**. We'll find a way together.*
We'll save, we'll plan and we'll heal as a family.
You're not a burden. You're our own. And we stand by you like a rock."

Because when you give this kind of emotional security to someone drowning in debt, you are **not just saving their finances you may be saving their life.**

Wisdom can come later.

But if life is lost, who will learn? Be the hand that holds. Not the hand that pushes.

Solutions that Communities can Offer:

- Conduct **financial literacy workshops** in urban and rural India.
- Normalize **talking about money stress** like any health issue.
- Create **community savings and support groups** for rural areas.
- Establish local **helplines for debt-related emotional support.**

Practical Solutions: What Banks *Can* Offer:

Loan Restructuring / Recasting

If someone has no income or extremely reduced income, they can approach the bank to restructure the loan, which may include:

- Reducing the EMI and increasing the loan tenure
- Temporarily converting a loan to interest-only payments
- Giving a grace period of 3–12 months before resuming EMIs

✅ RBI guidelines actually support restructuring under hardship cases (e.g., COVID-19 loan moratoriums were an example).

But most people don't know they can request it directly.

Moratorium Request (Pause the Loan Temporarily)

If there is zero income due to medical emergencies, job loss or personal crises, **you can request a moratorium** a period during which:

- You don't have to pay EMIs
- Interest may still accrue, but no penalties are charged
- No harassment or credit score damage happens during the pause

Many banks quietly accept such requests for **3 to 6 months**, especially if they are backed by proof and a written application.

One-Time Settlement (OTS)

For those in extreme distress:

- Banks can **offer a reduced lump sum** to close the loan
- **They may waive interest, penalties, or a portion of the principal**
- Some banks offer **zero-interest repayment plans for up to 12 months** as part of the settlement

This may affect your credit score but it saves your life, dignity and future.

Loan Closure via Insurance

Many personal loans and education loans come with **credit life insurance** or **loan protection cover** (knowingly or unknowingly signed at time of loan).

In case of:

- Disability
- Job loss
- Mental health breakdown (in some cases)

→ Check if the policy can help waive or pay off your loan. Most families don't even check this and end up bearing unnecessary trauma.

Credit Counseling by RBI-Approved Centers

There are **RBI-approved institutions** (like Disha Trust, Abhay Credit Counseling, etc.) that:

- Talk to banks on your behalf
- Create realistic repayment plans
- Can **negotiate for interest waiver or longer tenure**

This works especially well for poor or middle-class families facing harassment. You don't have to fight alone.

Asset-Based Settlements

If the borrower is willing to sell a small property, vehicle or gold:

- Banks often allow settlements using such collateral
- They may agree to write off the remaining if partial payment is made

You just need to speak openly and submit a hardship letter.

Declare Bankruptcy (Last Resort, but Legal)

If the loan amount is too huge and you have genuinely no way to repay. India has an Individual Bankruptcy process under the Insolvency and Bankruptcy Code (IBC).

This allows:

- Legal cancellation or restructure of loans
- Protection from mental harassment or arrest
- A second chance to rebuild life

It's a complex process but a legal life-saving path if all else fails.

LEGAL PATHWAYS TO RELIEF:

For borrowers trapped in a cycle of debt, legal options are available. Understanding these can offer hope:

- **DEBT RESTRUCTURING-** The insolvency and Bankruptcy Code (IBC) allows individuals to restructure their loans, reducing the financial burden.
- **CONSUMER PROTECTION LAWS-** Unethical recovery practices can be legally challenged. No borrower should tolerate harassment.
- **LEGAL AID SERVICES-** Many non-profit organizations offer free legal support to those struggling with debt.
- **MEDIATION & ARBITRATION-** In many cases, disputes with creditors can be resolved through mediation, avoiding lengthy legal battles.

These legal rights are not widely known. Spreading awareness can prevent borrowers from feeling trapped and powerless. Because in the end, the strength to rise is always within you. And when you choose to rise, you contribute to a world that believes in hope, courage and "SUICIDE-MUKT-BHARAT".

POINTS TO REMEMBER:

- **Shame is the Enemy, Not Debt:** Debt can be negotiated. Shame grows in silence. **Break the silence.**
- **Debt Counselling Exists- Use It:** Government and NGO-supported services can restructure loans or pause repayments.
- You are never out of options until you decide to disappear.
- **Avoid Illegal Lending Apps:** Check RBI-registered lenders. Most harassment comes from **unauthorized digital sharks.**
- **Involve Loved Ones, Don't Protect Them from the Truth:** When you share the weight, it gets lighter. They'll be hurt more by your absence than your honesty.
- **Make a Financial Survival Plan-One Step at a Time:** Prioritize essentials. Negotiate interest. Ask for moratoriums. You can start over.

- **Your Life Is Worth More Than Your Credit Score:** There are no graveyards for bad finances. But there are families broken by lost lives.

Don't become a memory over missed payment.

Mythological Insight:

1. King Harishchandra:

Known for his truthfulness, once lost everything his kingdom, his throne, his wealth to repay a debt to Sage Vishwamitra. Yet, he chose **dignity over hopelessness.**

He did not escape through death, though it would have been easier.

He worked at a cremation ground, collecting fees for funerals until the gods themselves had to return his kingdom in awe of his perseverance.

This ancient story is not about sacrifice. It's about grit in humiliation, about facing financial ruin without collapsing spiritually.

Harishchandra reminds us:

Even kings fall. But those who keep walking, rise again stronger, wiser and freer.

2. The Story of Sudama and Shri Krishna

Sudama, a childhood friend of Lord Krishna, was a poor Brahmin. He lived in extreme poverty so much that his children slept hungry and his wife had to remind him of his bond with Krishna to seek help. Ashamed and hesitant, Sudama carried a small bundle of flattened rice (*poha*) as a humble gift when he went to meet the king of Dwarka.

He never even asked for help.

But Krishna- the king washed his feet, embraced him with tears and gave him more wealth and respect than any royal could dream of. Not because of what Sudama had, but because of who he was.

What can we learn from this?

- Sudama didn't lose his **humility**, even in poverty.
- Krishna didn't measure his friend's worth by his **debt**, but by his
- heart.
- Help someone even before they ask, if you know, you know."

If You're Still Here, You're Winning

You might have shaky hands right now. Let them shake. It means your soul is still trying to hold on.

Just breathe.

Because your breath is **not borrowed.**

It is **divine.**

And the world is a better place with you in it.

From the Author's Heart to Yours:

Dear Reader,

If you're holding this book with trembling hands, unsure whether your tomorrow is worth fighting for. I want to speak to you, not as a writer, but as someone who sees your pain.

I don't know your exact numbers.

But I know how ***debt can make even breathing feel expensive.***

I know how it makes every door feel like it's closing in slow motion and every phone call feels like an alarm bell.

I know how you've hidden those loan messages, the late payment slips, the tears you cry quietly after pretending all day that you're "managing fine."

But I also want you to know this:

You are not your liabilities. You are not your lowest moment. You are not alone.

You are a universe of untold stories. You are someone's whole world.

This book wasn't written for applause. It was written for ***you*** *the one who still chooses to read, even while fighting battles nobody sees. If you're still here, reading these lines. You've already proved something extraordinary:* ***You're not done yet.***

Please stay.

Help exists.

Healing is possible.

And I promise you the world still needs your light, even if all you see right now is darkness.

With all my heart,

Anna (My Pen Name)

A Final Whisper Before the Door Closes:

If you're drowning in debt, this book sees you.

If you're hiding bills in shame, this chapter embraces you.

If you think it's the end, it's not. **It's a pause. Not a full stop.**

And if you're reading this and know someone in debt **call them. Now.**

Tell them they matter. You might save their life.

You are not alone.

You are loved. You are needed.

And you are still here and that's enough.

Now go ahead pick up the key and... **open Door 3.**

The conversation continues and so does your healing...

Key to Door 3

THIS KEY HOLDS A MESSAGE "NEVER GIVE UP"

This door brings back belief
HOPE
DOOR 3
THE SILENT SUICIDE BEHIND REPORT CARDS

The Silent Suicide Behind Report Cards

The Weight of Expectations: When Childhood Becomes a Battleground

THE NIGHT SHE ALMOST DIDN'T SEE TOMORROW:

A girl whose name was Aarya sat in the corner of her room, clutching the marksheet in her trembling hands. FAIL. The word stared back at her, mocking her dreams. This word 'FAIL' felt like a sharp knife to her heart. Tears blurred her vision.

Outside, the world had already started talking. "She was so confident...Now look at her!'

What a shame! She has ruined her family's name...

She should just disappear...Disappear...This word kept repeating in her mind. Maybe they were right. Maybe it was better if she was no longer here. That very night, while everyone was asleep, Aarya sat on her bed, holding a bottle of sleeping pills. If she took them all everything would end-No More Shame, No More Pain.

Just as she opened the bottle, there was a soft knock on her door. Aarya Beta...are you awake?

It was her mother. Her innocent voice broke her heart.

Aarya quickly wiped her tears and opened the door. And her mother walked in and hugged her. We love you beta 'she whispered before falling asleep beside her. She lay awake, staring at the ceiling. If I die, what will happen to my family? What will happen to my sisters? People will always poke them for my insane act.

There, she decided to live. But the pain didn't go away. Society still talked. People still pointed fingers. The shame was still there. Her relatives had always tried hard to demean her in every other way. As relatives kept on poking her; Aarya tried to commit suicide again- standing on the terrace, looking down. But then her father's voice called, Aarya come inside the house its cold out there. That care and warmth in his voice pulled Aarya back. But still suicidal tendencies were there in her mind because she was not able to handle that pressure of being labeled as a Failure.

And, then third time when she finally tried to kill herself...locking herself in the washroom with a blade in her hand. But then her sister started knocking the door and tried to stop her by saying................

"NO MATTER WHAT HAPPENS AARYA,
YOU ARE STILL OUR PRIDE"

Her hands shook. Tears rolled down her cheeks. Why do they still love me? Why don't they just hate me like everyone else does? And then she realized.... her family was not ashamed of her. "Society was," and who cares for what society thinks...her parents, her siblings- they loved her for who she was, not for her marks. That very night, she made a decision. NOT TO DIE, BUT TO RISE AGAIN.

Years passed, Aarya worked hard- not to prove society wrong, but to prove her family Right.

One day she stood on a big stage, holding prestigious award. The same people who once called her a failure were now clapping for her. She looked at her Parent's face, their eyes filled with happy tears. Her siblings, smiled proudly. "Aarya had Won". Not just an award, but her life.

Like Aarya, we must understand that society does not define us- our **WILL TO FIGHT does.**

Real-Life Case 1: The Last Attempt:

A boy from a middle-class family, 26, had given **five attempts** for a prestigious government exam. Each failure made him more silent.

His father mortgaged their land to pay for coaching and rent. His relatives stopped inviting him to weddings.

His friends moved on with jobs and marriages and he was stuck in an endless loop of mock tests and missed cut-offs.

He left a line behind:

"The exam failed me, yes. But the silence from everyone who loved me... that's what truly broke me."

When his father read the note, he kept repeating:

"Why didn't I tell him that we'd still love him... no matter what?"

But it was too late.

Real-Life Case 2: The Girl Who Couldn't Cross 33 Marks:

A 15-year-old girl in Class 10, failed in mathematics three times. Her school labelled her "weak," and her classmates whispered, "She's a waste of a seat."

No teacher offered help.

Her parents screamed more than they spoke. Eventually, she stopped trying... and stopped breathing.

Her brother found her suicide note:

"I was not stupid. I just needed someone to explain without anger."

What We Need to Understand:

- Failure in exams or interviews does not mean failure in life,
- unless we label it so.
- In India, *respect is conditional*: tied to results, marks, rankings and job offers.
- Repeated exam failures- especially in competitive and government exams create chronic shame, anxiety and identity loss.
- Families think they are motivating, but often they are **punishing with silence and pressure**.
- A child preparing for years in isolation, with no support, lives a life of *unseen suffering* full of fear, low self-worth and eventual burnout.

"It wasn't the failure that ended their life. It was the fear of not being enough." In today's highly competitive world, a child's worth is often measured by numbers- grades, percentage and ranking rather than by their values, dreams or emotional well-being. As a result, academic success has become the sole definition of a "bright future".. and failure has become a curse that many young hearts silently carry.

Every year in India, thousands of students die by suicide due to exam pressure, poor academic performance or the fear of disappointing their parents. These are not just statistics- these are stories of children who once laughed, dreamed and hoped. But somewhere between schoolbags and report cards, their silent cries went unheard. Many of them were not weak. They were simply tired- tired of unrealistic expectations, constant comparison, fear of failure and the absence of emotional support. When a child fails an exam, they are told they failed in life. But the truth is: Life doesn't end with marks- only our understanding does.

Because a child is not a rank. Not a grade. Not a number.

A child is a Life and no mark is even more valuable than that.

The Comparison Trap: When Love of Parents Becomes a Competition

A Letter to Every Loving Parent:

There is no love purer than a parent's love.

You carried them in your arms, fed them with your hands and watched their first steps with trembling joy. You stayed awake during their fevers and prayed silently during every exam. In your heart, you want only one thing: for your child to be happy, successful and safe.

But sometimes, without realizing it, love starts speaking the language of comparison. It begins to measure instead of embrace. And slowly, a child who once looked into your eyes with confidence begins to avoid your gaze. Not because they don't love you but because they're afraid they've disappointed you.

In the lives of many students, the greatest pressure doesn't always come from exams but from expectations. The subtle shift happens when love begins to feel like a reward for performance rather than a foundation of acceptance. For some, a parent's pride depends not only on how well they do but how much better they are than someone else. This is the comparison trap: where affection begins to feel conditional, self-worth is measured against others and emotional support is replaced by silent judgment. In this environment, love is no longer a source of security, it becomes a competition.

They remember the silence when they brought home an average score. They remember the pride in your voice when another child's name was mentioned. They remember how love felt more abundant when they were winning and how it quietly disappeared when they struggled.

They begin to believe:

"If I don't come first, I won't be loved first." "If I fail, I will lose them."

And in this emotional confusion, many children stop reaching out. Some fall into anxiety. Some isolate themselves. And a few, tragically, begin to wonder whether their absence would bring more peace than their presence.

This Is Not Your Fault. But It Is in Your Hands.

From Competition to Compassion: A New Model of Parenting:

Let us reimagine parenting not as a pursuit of perfection, but as a relationship rooted in compassion. Some alternative approaches include:

- Replacing "Why didn't you come first?" with "What did you learn
- this time?"
- Replacing "Look what others are doing" with "What do ***you*** enjoy
- doing?"
- Replacing silent disappointment with meaningful dialogue.

We dream of a nation where no child feels like ending their life because of a test, a rank, or a mistake. That dream starts at home with parents who choose connection over comparison.

Children naturally begin to show their best and become creative when they grow up in a positive and supportive home environment. A healthy family atmosphere can truly shape a child's bright future. As a parent, it's important to learn this- your child is not a project to perfect, but a soul to protect especially in today's challenging times."

That is how we build a Suicide Mukt Bharat one emotionally safe home at a time.

For Families of Students: Preparing for Govt Exams or Repeating Years

So many families say, "*Humne toh sab kuch de diya. (we gave everything we had)*.. But what students needed **most** wasn't just money. It was:

- A hug after failure
- Assurance that they are **still valued**
- Someone to silence the shame from neighbours and relatives If your son or daughter is breaking inside from repeated failures:
- Offer help before they ask.
- Say things like:

  "We'll find a way out."
  "Let's look at alternatives together."
  "You're not alone. You don't have to hide this pain."

When you offer this kind of strength, you don't just help them succeed...

You **save their life.**

Because if they live they can always learn. But if they die all your advice dies with them.

What Parents and Educators Must Understand:

- **Don't Wait for Them to Speak:** If your child or student suddenly becomes quiet, withdrawn, or 'too obedient,' pay attention. Silence is a symptom.
- **Create Space, Not Interrogation:** Sometimes students don't speak because every conversation feels like a lecture or a judgment. Be present. Be patient. Let silence be followed by warmth, not pressure.
- **Ask Gentle Questions:** Instead of asking, "What's wrong with you?"
- try asking:
- *"How have you been feeling these days?"*
- *"Is there something you wish you could talk about without fear?"*
- **Normalize Emotional Expression:** Speak about your own struggles, too. Vulnerability from adults makes it safer for children to open up.
- **Seek Professional Help When Needed:** Therapy or counselling is not a sign of failure, it's a gift of support.

✕ DON'Ts: What Parents Must Avoid

- Don't Compare Your Child to others: "Look at your cousin..."
- only creates shame, not improvement.
- Don't Use Fear or Threats: saying things like *"If you fail, what will people say?"* only increases anxiety and isolation.
- Don't dismiss or minimize Their Emotions: Phrases like *"It's not a big deal"* or *"Everyone goes through this"* can shut them down.
- Don't Label or Criticize Their Character: Avoid words like *"lazy,"* *"weak,"* or *"useless."* Attack the problem, not the person.

- Don't Ignore Warning Signs: Sudden silence, mood swings, withdrawal, or "I'm tired of everything" are not phases they are signals.

For Every Child Who Feels They're Failing: - what you *should* do?

- **Speak up When It Hurts:** Silence is not strength. Find one person- a parent, friend, teacher, or helpline and share your feelings.
- **Take Breaks Without Guilt:** your brain is not a machine. Rest is not laziness. It's fuel.
- **Focus on Effort, Not Just Outcome:** you don't control results, but
- you control your commitment. That's what builds growth.
- **Limit social media during Exams:** Seeing others "succeed" online is not reality...its highlights. Protect your focus and peace.
- **Create a Small Daily Routine:** Simple habits like waking up on time, staying hydrated, or journaling can give you a sense of control.
- **Ask for Academic Help When You're Stuck:** Struggling doesn't mean you're weak. It means you're learning. Seek support, not shame.
- **Remember: Exams Are Temporary:** One paper cannot decide your entire journey. Have a clear perspective.

DON'Ts - What You *Must* Avoid:

- **Don't Keep Emotions Bottled In:** Suppressed stress turns into anxiety or depression. Express before it overflows.
- **Don't Compare Yourself to Others:** Everyone has a different story, background. Your race is with yourself, not them.
- **Don't Tie Your Worth to Marks:** A score reflects your preparation, not your value as a person.

- **Don't Joke about Suicide or Self-Harm:** These aren't punchlines. If you're thinking about it even passingly, please reach out.
- **Don't starve or Overwork Yourself:** Skipping meals, pulling all-nighters, or punishing yourself will only harm your body and brain.
- **Don't Assume No One Cares:** Help exists. People want to listen. You are *not* alone, even if it feels that way.

Remember: Failing an exam is not the end. Ending your life is. Please never confuse the two.

Government Support and Schemes for Students in Distress:

Many students silently face fear of failure and financial burden but **you are not alone**. The government of India has recognized these struggles and introduced **initiatives to help you survive and feel supported.**

Scheme/Initiative	What It Offers	Whom It Helps
MANODARPAN (Ministry of Education)	Psychological support, helplines, expert counseling, online resources.	School & college students facing emotional stress, anxiety or pressure.
National Toll-Free Helpline – 8448440632	Free, confidential mental health counseling from trained psychologists.	Students, parents and teachers.
Vidya Lakshmi Portal	Single-window access to **student education loans** and scholarships.	Students needing financial support for college/technical education.
SWAYAM Portal	Free online courses by IITs, IIMs and UGC-recognized universities.	Students struggling academically or wanting low-cost learning.

PM CARES for Children	Financial and emotional support for children orphaned during COVID-19.	Children who lost both parents and need educational aid.
Scholarships (NSP Portal)	Scholarships for SC/ST/OBC/Minorities and merit-based/need-based support.	Economically weaker students pursuing higher studies.

These schemes are **not just names on a list** they're lifelines created for **you.** If you're drowning in pressure, unable to afford education, or thinking you're a failure **please reach out**. Real people and real change are waiting for you.

Mythological Insight:

Goddess Saraswati & the Forgotten Path

In Indian mythology, **Goddess Saraswati** is the divine embodiment of knowledge, learning and wisdom but what most forget is that she **never** demanded perfection. Her blessings were not reserved only for toppers or scholars, but for seekers anyone who pursued knowledge with sincerity.

When **Valmiki,** once a thief and an uneducated man, was guided by "Sage Narada" to chant the name of Rama, he couldn't even pronounce it properly. Instead of chanting Rama...Rama..He repeated it backward-"Mara... Mara..." and yet, through **his intent and his transformation,** he was blessed. That same man went on to write the Ramayana, one of the greatest epics ever known.

Saraswati shows us that **true learning isn't about marks** it's about inner evolution. **The student who fails ten times but gets up eleven is closer to wisdom than the one who only knows answers on a sheet.**

Let this be a reminder:

If the doors of colleges close, knock on the doors of character. If degrees deny you, let dignity define you.

You don't need to be the best... you only need to keep seeking, keep rising.

As you step out of this door, reader, I want you to know this:

You are not your exam results. You are not your rejections. You are not the silence in your room after a tough day. You are a story still unfolding. There are colleges you haven't discovered, skills you haven't unlocked and moments of joy you haven't lived yet. You just walked through a door filled with pressure ...silent suffering.

But as you leave, I hope your heart carries something stronger the unshakable belief that your life matters.

If **Door 3** made even one parent stop before comparing their child's worth

to someone else's marks,
If it gave even one student the courage to speak instead of staying silent, if it helped even one family find the words to say, *"No matter what, we're standing by you,"*

Then this Door has opened more than a path....it has opened hearts.

And if it reached **you**, dear reader then may you walk ahead not just informed, but transformed.

Remember my words:

You are not alone. You were never meant to be.

Key to Door 4

THIS KEY OPENS THE DOOR TO "LETTING GO"

DOOR 4
NEW HOPE

The Goodbye that Broke Me

The Silence After Goodbye:
When Grief Becomes Too Loud

She didn't scream.

She didn't leave a note.

She just sat with a photo of her father in her lap... and stopped breathing.

Some absences don't echo. They crush.

This door isn't about failure.

It is about loss so personal, so profound, that the heart forgets how to beat without the one it loved.

When Someone You Love Becomes a Memory

How do you live in a house where every corner smells of your mother's prayer shawl?

How do you sit on a dining table chair that was once filled by your father's laughter?

How do you open your eyes in the morning when the first face you searched for is no longer in this world?

Some people don't die. They take a part of us with them.

And in that hollowness, many begin to lose the will to go on. Some don't eat. Some don't sleep.

Some stare at their phones wishing the impossible. And some... jump, hang, overdose, or disappear.

Grief Has Many Faces:

- **A child who keeps waiting at the window**, not yet old enough to understand that their parents are never coming back. Their world turns quiet, their laughter fades and no one hears the questions they carry inside.
- **An elderly person who wakes up to an empty side of the bed** after spending decades holding the same hand. Now, loneliness echoes in every corner of the house and silence becomes heavier than words.
- **A young couple, torn apart too soon one left behind**, living a life that feels like emotional death.

  They walk through routines, but nothing feels real anymore. Every dream shared now feels like a memory carved in pain.
- **Siblings who lose their brother or sister**-their childhood partner in crime, their shadow, their mirror. And as they stand beside a coffin, something in them breaks that will never be whole again.
- **Families drowning in guilt**... whispering "If only we had seen the signs," "If only we had reached sooner," "If only we had listened."

They replay every moment, every word and every missed opportunity over and over again.

Grief doesn't always come with tears. Sometimes it walks quietly, sits beside us and lives within us. It wears many faces all equally human. All equally sacred

The Trauma of Witnessing Death

Some people don't just mourn a loved one.

They see them die.

They hold their hands as the light leaves their eyes.

They wait in ambulance lines, ICU benches, crematoriums.

And this trauma?

It becomes an invisible wound. A slow poison.

Leading to anxiety, depression, PTSD and in some cases... suicide.

All these relationships. All these aching situations.

They don't just teach us how people die...

They teach us what it truly means to live

- When a child loses their parents, we learn that love isn't guaranteed to last forever and that even the smallest shoulders can carry the heaviest pain.

  It teaches us to hold our children closer, speak gentler and never leave love unspoken.

- When an old man stares at the empty chair where his wife once sat, we realize that time is fragile. That no matter how long we're together, it's never long enough.

  It teaches us to treasure shared silence, to listen more deeply and to grow old with gratitude, not regret.

- When a young partner is left behind, walking through life without the one they dreamed with, we understand that love is not just about being together it's about *surviving even after one heart stops beating.*

  It teaches us that grief is the price of deep love and yet, we still choose to love anyway.

- When siblings weep at a funeral, we're reminded that the people who know us best can be taken in a moment.

  It teaches us to forgive faster, laugh louder and never assume there's more time.

And when families crumble in guilt, whispering "if only...",
it teaches us the most haunting lesson of all:
See people while they're still alive.
Listen before it's too late.
Love them now- not just in eulogies.

These situations soaked in sorrow are not just tragedies.
They are lessons carved in pain that whisper to the living.
Be kind. Be present. Be aware.
Because every goodbye might be the last.

And maybe, just maybe, if we learn from their stories,
we won't have to write our own in grief.

Dear Reader, You Who Are in Pain...

I know.

You're not weak. You just loved deeply.

And when love leaves whether by fate or by choice the world loses its color.

But I want to ask you something, gently

If they are gone... should you go too?

Would your mother, if watching from somewhere, want to see you destroy the very life she once gave you?

Would your partner, who you loved so dearly, want your story to end like this?

Would your child even if gone want their parent to vanish in agony? No.

If you're reading this with tears, with shaking hands, with a chest full of ache **you are not alone.**

This chapter is written for you. This door was built for you.

Let's walk through it... together.

What Can Be Done: Practical & Powerful Solutions

- **Acknowledge the Grief- Don't Suppress It:** Grieving is not weakness. Cry. Write. Talk. Let yourself feel. You're not broken. You're healing.
- **Speak to a Professional:** Counselors and therapists help navigate loss. EMDR, trauma therapy, or even support groups are lifesavers.
- **Connect with Grief Circles or Communities:** Platforms like Grief India Movement, 1Life Foundation, iCall, Snehi, etc., help people heal together.
- **Channel Pain into Purpose:** Start a foundation in their name. Donate books. Adopt a cause they loved. Let their memory become your mission.
- **Rebuild Routine Slowly:** Bathing, eating, walking, talking may feel meaningless. But restart one by one. **Routines rebuild life.**
- **Avoid Substance Dependence**: Alcohol, sleeping pills and drugs
- **worsen grief.** Choose therapy over toxicity.
- **Let Someone In:** Even one friend who listens. Even one neighbor who understands. Even one therapist who reminds you: "Your life is still worth something."
- **Honor Their Memory with Life, Not Death:** They're gone. But what if your survival is their biggest tribute?

Government Schemes That Offer Hope:

For Widows/Widowers/Orphans:

- **National Family Benefit Scheme (NFBS):** ₹20,000 one-time grant if main breadwinner dies.
- Indira Gandhi National Widow Pension Scheme (IGNWPS):
- Monthly pension for widows aged 40-59.

- **Widow Remarriage Schemes** (in states like Maharashtra, Haryana): Financial support to rebuild lives.
- **Orphan Grant Schemes:** Financial aid for children who've lost parents.
- **Senior Citizen Pension Scheme:** For those left behind in old age.
- **Free Mental Health Counseling** through government hospitals under DMHP (District Mental Health Program).

Real Stories of Turning Grief into Grace:

1. **Dr. Abdul Kalam's Nephew- a Life beyond Loss:** After the sudden demise of Dr. A.P.J. Abdul Kalam, his nephew **Srijan Pal Singh**, who was also his close associate, was devastated. But instead of giving in to the void, he carried forward Dr. Kalam's vision through education missions, youth empowerment and launching the *Kalam Foundation*. He says, *"I didn't lose him. I became a part of him."*

2. **Anonymous: R,- Widow Turned Warrior:** Ruchi lost her husband, a young IPS officer, to a fatal accident. Grief crushed her, but her two daughters gave her strength. She studied law, fought legal battles for accident victims and today runs a support group for widows called Second Sunrise.

   She says, "His death didn't end my story. It gave me a reason to write a new one."

3. **Late Major Vikram Batra's Twin Brother- Love Lives On:** When Kargil war hero Major Vikram Batra died at 24, his twin brother **Vishal Batra** was shattered. But he dedicated his life to carrying Vikram's bravery forward. Today, Vishal speaks across India on love and loss keeping his brother alive in every heartbeat.

   He says, "I lost my twin, but gained the whole nation as a brotherhood."

These stories are not of superheroes.

They are of people...

...who chose to live, when death seemed easier.

If they can make it through the darkest tunnels of loss maybe, just maybe- so can you.

Let their stories sit beside yours in this Door. Let their strength touch your tears.

And let your survival be the next inspiring tale someone else needs.

Three very basic Healing techniques anyone can try:

1. The Lamp of Memory

Every evening, light a small lamp or candle in your home for 7 or 21 days. This is not just a ritual, it's a quiet moment of connection.

Sit near the light for a few minutes. Close your eyes and think about your loved one.

Talk to them in your heart. Tell them how your day was, how you feel, what you miss.

Keep a flower, photo, or anything that reminds you of them next to the lamp.

Say softly:

"You are still with me. I will live not just survive. For you and for me."

This simple act brings comfort and helps your heart heal without forgetting the love.

2. Letters to the One You Lost

Get a notebook and start writing letters to the person who is no longer here. Write like you are speaking to them.

Say everything you wish you had said your regrets, your gratitude and your love.

No one else needs to read these. This is for your heart.

Even if you cry while writing, let it flow. With each letter, the weight in your chest will get lighter.

Grief that is expressed starts to heal. What stays inside becomes pain. So let the pen carry your feelings.

3. Do One Small Thing They'd Be Proud Of

Think of something they would have loved to see you do something that

would've made them smile.

Maybe you continue your studies, take care of someone else, cook their favorite meal, or simply take a walk to feel better.

Even a small act counts. Say to yourself:

"They would want me to live, to laugh and to try again."

When you do something in their name, their love becomes your strength. It doesn't erase the pain, but it gives you a reason to move forward.

Mythological Insight:

- **Even Mahadev Shiv Grieved:** When Sati gave up her life after being insulted by her father, Lord Shiva was consumed by sorrow. He carried her body across the universe, his heart shattered and his silence louder than any storm.

  The grief didn't make him weaker it made him pause and retreat within. Through that deep pain, he found a new path not by forgetting her, but by honoring her with stillness, strength and purpose.

  If Shiva, the embodiment of divinity, could fall under the weight of love lost, so can you.

  And like him you can rise.

  Not by erasing the pain, but by carrying it with grace.

To smile again is not betrayal. It is your soul whispering: "I am still alive and I still love."

- **Abhimanyu's Death: The divine who could see the future but couldn't stop the loss.**

  Abhimanyu, Arjuna's son and Krishna's beloved nephew, was killed brutally in the Chakravyuh during the Kurukshetra war. Though Krishna could foresee it, **he allowed destiny to unfold.**

He cried silently not as a god, but as a family member.

He later became the guiding light for Uttara (Abhimanyu's wife) and ensured their unborn child, Parikshit, lived on.

Insight: Sometimes, even God allows pain to happen, not because he is cruel, but because from that pain will rise the next protector.

Loss, then, is not an end but a painful beginning of new life.

If this Door has made even one grieving heart believe they can smile again...

If it has made even one parent speak softer to their child... If it has made even one broken soul hold on one more day... Then this Door has served its sacred purpose.

You're still here. You're still breathing.

There's life ahead of you.

And it is beautiful.

Just like the love you lost. Hold it. Honor it. Live for it.

Exit Door 4. Come and pick Key 5.

Key to Door 5

THIS KEY SHELTERS YOU FROM PAST STORMS

DOOR 5
YOU
ARE NOT
ALONE

She Broke Quietly

The Burden Women Are Told to Carry

Opening the Door: A Cry from Within Walls

In the corner of a dimly lit room, she sat with tears dried on her face, a photo of her wedding day in her lap. What once was joy, turned into quiet suffering. Her name was *Neelam*. After marriage, she became invisible except when dowry demands weren't met, or when she was blamed for giving birth to a daughter.

Each slap was followed by silence. Each taunt dripped with the poison of entitlement. She did everything right. Cooked. Cleaned. Smiled. Prayed for a child. But when the womb didn't bloom fast enough, the whispers turned to shouts. Her worth reduced to her fertility. Her dignity tied to a dowry.

That evening, her daughter found her swinging silently from the fan. A child holding a sari knot in her hand, asking her unconscious mother to wake up. But no answer came.

She was only 28.

Real Stories That Never Made Headlines

- A 26-year-old bride from Haryana hung herself just 5 months after marriage. Her note said: "No one beats me here. But no one sees me either."
- A young woman in Karnataka was blamed for not conceiving. Her mother-in-law reportedly said, "We brought in a barren daughter-in-law." She consumed poison during Diwali celebrations while the family danced outside.

- In a corporate office in Mumbai, a woman facing constant sexual harassment by her manager was told by HR to "let it go or switch teams quietly." She jumped off her office terrace the next week.

These aren't stories. These are scars on a nation's soul.

The Unseen Wounds:

In the corners of countless Indian homes, women cry themselves to sleep. Not because they're weak, but because no one listens.

A woman arrives in a new family with dreams in her eyes only to be met with cold silences. In some households, the in-laws refuse to speak with the new bride altogether. No confrontation, just indifference. It's a kind of quiet that shatters more brutally than words ever could.

Silent treatment is not silence. It's slow, invisible violence.

Women lose their will to live not just due to one slap, one demand for dowry, or one cruel word. But due to the thousands of daily moments where they are made to feel less than human. When no one stands up for them. When they're told to "adjust." When their worth is reduced to their womb, their cooking, their obedience.

The Burdens She's Forced to Carry:

- Dowry-related harassment that begins subtly and ends in brutality.
- Pressure to conceive
- Blame and shame for giving birth to a girl child.
- In-law interference in her decisions, clothing, time, identity.
- Workplace harassment where colleagues become predators.
- Trauma of sexual assault or rape with no one to talk to.
- Forced isolation denied visits to her parents, friends, or support.

- Public defamation through character assassination or slander.
- Domestic violence hidden behind closed doors.
- Fear of custody loss that keeps women trapped in violent marriages.

These few problems we've written are just the tip of the iceberg. Countless women silently endure far more every day, some ending their lives, while others continue to suffer in silence for a lifetime.

What Can Women Do? Practical & Legal Solutions

1. **Talk about the Silence:** If your in-laws are refusing to acknowledge you, ask respectfully: "Is there something I can do to bridge this?" Start the conversation they refuse to have.
2. **Set Boundaries Early:** It's not rebellion. It's self-respect. Define what kind of behavior you will not tolerate be it emotional manipulation or forced sacrifices.
3. **Document Everything:** Keep a record of dowry demands, emotional abuse, or threatening texts. This is crucial for legal protection.
4. **Know Your Rights Under Indian Law:**
   - Section 498A IPC: Protects against cruelty by husband or his family.
   - Protection of Women from Domestic Violence Act, 2005: Safeguards women from physical, sexual, emotional, verbal and economic abuse.
   - Sexual Harassment of Women at Workplace (Prevention, Prohibition and Redressal) Act, 2013: Guarantees a safe work environment.
   - The Pre-Conception and Pre-Natal Diagnostic Techniques Act: Prevents sex-selective abortions and protects the rights of girl children.

5. **Reach Out Without Shame:**
   - Call **181...**Women's Helpline (national).
   - Contact **NCW (National Commission for Women)** for complaints and legal aid.
   - Approach **Legal Aid Clinics** for free legal consultation in your city.
6. **Train in Self-Defense:**
   - Enroll in Krav Maga, Taekwondo, or any martial art that builds reflex, balance and self-confidence. Physical readiness often builds emotional courage.
7. **Build a Personal Support System:**
   - Create a circle of trusted friends, family, or even online communities. One voice saying "I believe you" can be life-saving.
8. **Therapy Is Strength, Not Shame:**
   - Healing from trauma takes professional help. Don't hesitate to consult a trauma-informed psychologist or counselor.
9. **Start Financial Independence:**
   - Explore online work, remote jobs, or skills like teaching, designing or writing. Financial power is freedom.

When Love Turns into Betrayal- Coping with a Husband's

Extramarital Affair and Divorce

"He promised forever... but chose someone else midway. The marriage ended not just in court, but in the deepest corners of her soul. Divorce came like a stamp on her wound not her fault, but still her scar. She didn't die because he left... she almost died wondering why she wasn't enough."

In Indian households, we teach girls to fight for love, adjust endlessly and tolerate everything even betrayal all in the name of saving the marriage.

But what happens when the marriage cannot be saved because **the betrayal** is so deep, it burns the woman's self-worth to ashes. Today, thousands of women in India and around the world fall into **emotional trauma, severe depression** and suicidal thoughts after discovering that their husbands have been cheating emotionally, physically or digitally.

They don't just feel abandoned. They feel replaced.

Real Impact of Betrayal:

- **Severe Emotional Trauma:** The shock of betrayal often leads to PTSD-like symptoms.
- **Identity Loss:** "Am I not beautiful enough? Good enough? Worth
- loving?"
- **Family Shame:** Society still blames the woman for a broken marriage, even when it wasn't her fault.
- **Isolation:** Friends, in-laws, or relatives often distance themselves.
- **Financial Dependency:** Many women feel trapped if they have no income or support system.
- **Childcare Pressure:** Mothers fear how to raise their children alone. And in all this pain, one thought keeps haunting them:

"Maybe it would've been better if I just didn't exist."

But **NO.** You are not here to be broken by someone else's wrong. You are here to rise above it, with strength and unshakable dignity.

Practical Solutions:

1. **Pause Before You React....Choose Yourself First**

   - Don't make a permanent decision (like suicide) in response to someone else's temporary disloyalty.

- Step away from the chaos. Take time to breathe, cry and **let it hurt** but don't let it destroy you.

Pain is a signal to heal, not to end.

2. **Seek Emotional & Psychological Support**

- Talk to a **therapist or counselor** who is experienced in relationship trauma or betrayal.
- Consider joining a **support group** (online or offline) for women
- who've experienced infidelity.
- Practice **journaling, expressive writing,** or audio recordings of your feelings your voice deserves to be heard.

3. **Know Your Rights**

- In India, if the affair causes mental cruelty, it can be used as grounds for **divorce** under Section 13 of the Hindu Marriage Act.
- If the cheating involves misuse of finances or coercion, **legal recourse** is available. Speak to a women's rights lawyer.
- **Child custody, alimony** and **financial support** can still be claimed don't let financial fear trap you.

You are not powerless. The law can be your shield, use it if needed.

4. **Do Not Isolate Yourself**

- Share your pain with **at least one trusted person** a sister, mother, friend or mentor.
- Do not keep secrets that are destroying you inside. Silence is not strength when it's suffocating you.

5. **Reclaim Your Identity**

- Rediscover old passions art, work, reading, dance, cooking or anything that once made you *feel calm*.

- Enroll in a **new skill, course, or job**...financial independence boosts self-respect.
- Look in the mirror and say every day:

"I am not just someone's wife. I am someone's whole world including mine."

6. **Protect Your Children (If Any)**
   - Your children learn strength from watching you.
   - Choose healing not bitterness. Speak respectfully about their father, but **teach them self-worth, loyalty and emotional boundaries.**
7. **Spiritual Grounding**
   - Turn inward. Chant, pray, meditate, or simply sit in silence daily to build mental strength.
   - Read scriptures, self-help books, or mythological stories of strong women like Draupadi, Sita, or Meera Bai, who found light in betrayal and pain.
8. **Set Boundaries**
   - You don't have to forgive instantly or pretend everything is okay.
   - You also don't have to take revenge.
   - Learn to say:

"I may still be in this house, but I now live with awareness, self-respect and clarity."

9. **Create a Future You're Proud Of**
   - Whether you choose to stay or walk away...let it be **your choice,**
   - not the pain's command.
   - One day, you will look back and be proud that **you chose yourself when no one else did.**

Government Schemes Supporting Women

- **Ujjawala Scheme:** For women rescued from trafficking or abuse.
- **Mahila Shakti Kendra:** Empowerment and legal guidance at the grassroots.
- **Nirbhaya Fund:** Victim support for survivors of sexual abuse.
- **One-Stop Centers (OSC):** Provide medical, legal and counseling aid under one roof.
- **Sukanya Samriddhi Yojana:** Secure your girl child's future savings.
- **Working Women Hostels:** Safe, subsidized accommodations for employed women.

Mythological Insight

In the **Ramayana**, Sita's strength was not just in enduring exile but in returning with dignity. When abandoned unjustly, she raised her sons alone, never seeking revenge but standing tall in dharma.

Let every woman remember: You are not just someone's wife, daughter-in-law, or mother. You are a force of creation.

When a Crime Steals Dignity But Not Her Worth: A Rape Survivor

*Some women never make it past the trauma of **Rape** not because they're weak, but because society often makes them feel as if they should be ashamed, as if it was their fault, as if their future has ended.*

The world often fails these women **twice**:

First, when the violation happened.

Second, when they were made to carry the shame instead of the rapist. A girl in her early 20s once whispered in a suicide note:

"I wasn't afraid of what happened to me...
I was afraid of how the world would look at me after.

This is not just her story. This is the cruel silence many rape survivors are buried in.

Why Some Women Choose Death After Rape:

- **Fear of blame** by family or community.
- **Social stigma**: Being seen as "impure" or "broken."
- **Victim shaming** even in police stations or courts.
- **Media trials** and lack of privacy.
- **Marriage prospects** being destroyed.
- **No safe space to heal**, mentally or physically.

Some women feel so contaminated by society's hate, they believe they no longer belong to this world. That belief is a **lie** the world has fed them. And that **lie is killing them.**

What Must Be Done- For Survivors of Rape

1. **Shift the Shame Back Where It Belongs**
   - The survivor is not dirty. The crime is. The rapist is.
   - As a society, we must stop asking *"What was she wearing?"* and start asking *"Why did he do this?"*
2. **Medical & Legal First Steps**
   - Immediate medical attention for physical and forensic care.

- File an FIR under Section 376 IPC (Indian Penal Code).
- Request for a lady officer at the police station.
- Access free treatment under the Nirbhaya Fund.

3. **Psychological Support**
   - Counseling is **not optional**- it's necessary.
   - Govt and NGOs like **SAARTHAK, Rape Crisis Centers & One-Stop Centers** offer free psychological aid.
4. **Rehabilitation and Dignity Restoration**
   - Stop hiding the survivor. Give her a life of employment and visibility.
   - Empower her through skill-building programs, educational support.
5. **Support from Families and Partners**
   - Stand **with** her, not **behind** her in shame.
   - Tell her: *"You were never the reason. We love you. We're proud of your strength."*
6. **Legal Aid**
   - Victim compensation schemes are available in every state.
   - Free legal aid via **District Legal Services Authority** (DLSA).

Before you step out of this Door, as the author, I offer a heartfelt salute to those brave souls who endured the horror of sexual violence.

To those who lost their lives to that trauma my heart grieves for you.

But to the ones still choosing life despite the scars...you are strength personified.

This chapter, these words, are my small tribute to your unbreakable spirit. You didn't just survive you've become a light of courage and hope for countless others.

Mythological Parallel:

Even in mythology, women have faced grave violation; Draupadi's disrobing stands as a symbol of humiliation. But what did she do? She did not hide. She did not accept the shame.

She called upon the divine and she rose. Her voice echoed through history.

Let modern women know: Your voice matters. Your life matters more than your shame.

You are not what happened to you.

You are what you choose to become after.

To Every Survivor

Please read this as if I'm sitting in front of you:

Your life is not ruined.

You are not "less than."

You don't need to disappear to be believed. Stay. Not for them. For you.

Because the crime ends the day they are punished, not the day you disappear.

As you step out of this Door, may you carry not the weight of what broke you but the fire of what you chose to rise from.

You are not defined by their silence or their expectations. You are defined by your courage.

Walk ahead because ***You Matter.***

Time to pick Key 6

Key to Door 6

THIS KEY REMINDS: HE MATTERS BEYOND HIS DUTIES

DOOR 6
BREAKING THE SILENCE ON MEN'S MENTAL HEALTH

"HE" Was Never Allowed to Break

When Men Cry Silently

The Pain No One Talks About

We speak of feminism, empowerment and equality. But in the process, we've often forgotten to talk about the **quiet suffering of men**. The fathers who provide without complaint. The sons who bury their dreams to fulfill duties. The brothers who absorb pressure but never express pain. The husbands who remain unheard even in their own homes.

This is not about comparison. This is not about silencing one voice to raise another. This is about acknowledging **the pain that men carry silently,** the weight that often leads them to one fatal decision: **to end it all.**

Why Do Men Take Their Own Lives?

Here are **the real reasons** men die by suicide reasons society still hesitates to accept:

- **The Burden of Being the Breadwinner:** Even when unemployed or financially weak, men are still expected to "figure it out."
- **No Space to Express Emotion:** From childhood, boys are told
- "Men aren't supposed to feel pain." Crying is considered weakness.
- **Neglect in Relationships:** Many men suffer emotional neglect from their partners or families and they are never asked, "How are *you* really doing?"
- **Constant Judgment:** Men are judged on their bank balance, job title and ability to provide even when they're emotionally or physically struggling.

- **Victims of Domestic** Abuse: Yes, men face abuse too. But when they speak up, they're mocked.
- **False Allegations:** Dowry laws, workplace harassment accusations, or child custody battles often become traps that ruin innocent lives.
- **Lack of Emotional Support:** Unlike women, most men don't have a close circle to vent or heal.
- **Suicidal Loneliness in Divorce or Breakups:** Many men are left shattered after the loss of a relationship but are expected to "move on like a man."
- Sexual abuse (yes, even that): Men are sexually abused too, especially in childhood but most never talk about it.
- **Pressure to Stay Strong All the Time:** Even when they want to collapse, society expects them to hold everything together.

When a Man Breaks Inside: The Untold Pain of Betrayal and Divorce

In today's evolving world, not all men are wrong and not all women are victims.

There are countless men gentle, loyal, supportive husbands who have been shattered by betrayal, falsely accused and left in silence to fight the emotional or legal wars of a failed marriage.

They don't speak.

Because society teaches them: "Men don't suffer."

But they do.

when they do their dignity, is bruised but they're expected to walk...

as if nothing happened."

When Love Becomes a Weapon:

There are those who come home one day only to find the woman they loved now loves someone else.

Some stumble upon hidden chats, unknown numbers or a growing silence and it shatters them from within.

And when they try to seek answers, they're told:

"Don't control me."

"Maybe it's your fault I looked elsewhere."

In many cases, the betrayal is followed by threats of divorce not just to leave but to extract **alimony, property, custody** and **dignity.**

They are painted black in courts. Called abusive without proof.

Stripped of fatherhood and self-worth. They are alive... but slowly dying inside.

Real-Life Echoes

Anonymous, a 34-year-old man from, found out his wife was having an affair with a colleague.

When he confronted her, she filed a case under Section 498A (dowry harassment) and demanded ₹25 lakhs to settle.

He lost his job, respect in his neighborhood and nearly ended his life.

He now attends therapy and mentors other men facing similar emotional trauma.

Anonymous IT professional, Bengaluru: "My wife left me and took my 3-year-old daughter with her. She didn't want me anymore, but still demanded a huge alimony. I cry every night not for her, but for the lullabies I can no longer sing to my daughter."

Practical Solutions: Standing Tall Again

1. **Seek Legal Help Immediately**
    - Don't suffer in silence. Hire a good family lawyer who has experience in false allegation defense.
    - Laws like **Section 498A, Domestic Violence Act and maintenance laws** can be misused but there are safeguards.
    - **You can file for child custody, visitation rights and legal protection from harassment.**
2. **Start Therapy-You Are Not Weak**
    - Many men hesitate to take therapy. But remember: your pain is valid.
    - Therapy helps you detach with dignity, manage anger, rebuild confidence and handle legal pressure emotionally.
3. **Join Men Support Communities**
    - Organizations like **Save Indian Family Foundation (SIFF)** offer legal and emotional support to falsely accused men.
    - Talking to someone who understands what you're going through
    - can save your life.
4. **Document Everything**
    - Maintain digital records, texts, emails, financial transactions.
    - False accusations can't stand where truth has strong evidence.
5. **Focus on Your Health & Career**

    Betrayal is real. But so is recovery. Channel your pain into physical fitness, upgrading your skills and reinventing your purpose.

Legal Protections and Remedies for Men in India (if wife is cheating or misusing the law)

1. **Adultery by Wife (Grounds for Divorce)**
   - Under **Section 13(1)(i) of the Hindu Marriage Act, 1955**, a man can file for divorce if he can prove that his wife had voluntary sexual relations outside the marriage.
   - Though **adultery is no longer a criminal offense (decriminalized by Supreme Court in 2018),** it still remains a valid **ground for divorce**.
2. **Protection from False 498A (Dowry) Cases**
   - Section 498A of IPC has been misused in some cases.
   - In Rajesh Sharma v. State of U.P. (2017), the Supreme Court directed that Family Welfare Committees must be formed to investigate 498A complaints before arrest.
   - Men falsely accused can seek anticipatory bail and file for quashing of FIR under Section 482 CrPC.
3. **Alimony Isn't Automatic**
   - A wife **is not automatically entitled to alimony.** Courts check:
     - Her financial status
     - Whether she is working
     - Whether the husband is financially capable
   - If the wife is at fault (e.g., adultery), courts may deny alimony.
4. **Child Custody Isn't Always the Mother's Right**
   - Courts decide custody based on the child's welfare, not just gender.
   - If the mother is proven unfit, or negligent, the father can be granted full custody after 5 years of age of the child.

5. **Property Rights**

   - A wife has no automatic right over husband's ancestral property.
   - She can claim **maintenance or share in marital property,** not property gifted by husband's family.
   - Men can protect their property by:
     - Not keeping assets in joint name unless necessary
     - Creating a **will**
     - Documenting every financial transaction.

Useful Legal Tools for Men:

1. **Right to Information (RTI) Act:** If a man is falsely accused or needs to gather proof of his innocence, he can file an RTI to obtain relevant documents or evidence from government departments, police records or hospitals.
2. **Section 9 of the Hindu Marriage Act- Restitution of Conjugal Rights:** If a wife leaves the husband without valid reason and he still wishes to reconcile or bring her back home, he can file a petition under Section 9. This helps show the court that he has tried to save the marriage.
3. **Section 21B of the Hindu Marriage Act (Fast Track for Divorce Proceedings):** This section allows men (or women) to request a speedy trial for divorce, especially if the case is dragging for years and affecting their mental and emotional health.
4. **Section 65B of the Indian Evidence Act:** Men can use digital and electronic evidence such as WhatsApp chats, call recordings, emails, CCTV footage as admissible proof in court to support their claims (for example, to prove extra-marital affair or false allegations).

Organizations That Help Men Legally:

- **Save Indian Family Foundation (SIFF)**: Provides free legal counseling to men suffering false allegations or marital abuse. Website: www.saveindianfamily.org
- **Men Welfare Trust**: Offers mental health, legal and family court support for men.
- **Vaastav Foundation:** Works for gender-neutral laws and legal awareness for men.

What Government Needs to Do (Still in Progress)

- Gender-Neutral Domestic Violence Law
- Helplines for Distressed Husbands
- **False Case Penalties:** Increase fines or jail for misuse of dowry or harassment laws.

Psychological Solutions for Men:

1. **Men's Mental Health Helplines:** Encourage men to use available suicide prevention and counseling services without shame.
2. **Create Male Safe Spaces:** Support or create groups (online or local) where men can speak freely and feel heard.
3. **Therapy Without Shame:** Men need to be told therapy isn't
4. weakness. It's self-respect.
5. **Know Your Legal Rights:**

- In false dowry or domestic cases, Section 498A must be challenged legally.
- Child custody rights are evolving, fathers now have a voice.

6. **Financial Guidance for Jobless or Pressured Men:** Seek government skill-training schemes, mental health support, or startup grants.
7. **Encourage Emotional Expression:** Families, especially mothers and wives, must stop expecting their sons or husbands to be "always strong."
8. **Educate Boys Differently:** Let young boys know crying is human. Teach them emotions are not shameful.
9. **Avoid Toxic Friendships:** Men often face mocking within male circles. Break free from such environments.
10. **Let Go of Pride to Seek Help:** Even if it means anonymous therapy, go for it. Pride should never cost life.
11. **For Women Reading This:** If you have a brother, partner, or father **ask him if he's okay, truly okay.** That one question might save his life.

Mythological Insight:

❖ Lord Ram- The Weight of Being "The Man"

In the pages of our epics, Lord Ram is often seen as the perfect son, the noble king, the valiant warrior.

But rarely do we speak of the **burden** he silently carried. **The pressure to uphold everyone's expectations, even if it crushed his own heart.**

To be "Ram" wasn't just a name it was a **duty that demanded unimaginable sacrifice.**

He left the throne for his father's promise.

He lived in exile for 14 years without complaint.

He bore deep wounds in silence not because he felt no pain, but because the world never gave him the space to grieve.

Lord Ram didn't cry in front of everyone.

But that didn't mean he didn't break from within.

Still, he stood. For his people. For his family. For dharma. This is the unseen pain men carry even today.

They smile and go to work they provide and protect,

They remain "strong" even when they are falling apart inside. Because **they're expected to.**

Lord Ram's Agni Pariksha Isn't Just Sita's Story

In the Ramayan, many focus only on Sita's Agni Pariksha but Ram too, suffered in silence, torn between dharma and love, blamed by people despite his righteousness. He gave up his beloved, not out of cruelty, but out of helpless **duty** just as many men today walk away with a heart dripping with sorrow, simply to protect others' respect.

Even men break. But like Ram, their story rarely gets understood.

❖ Bhishma- The Man Who Gave Up Everything

Bhishma Pitamah made a vow.....**a vow of celibacy and lifelong service**, just so his father could marry again.

- He sacrificed marriage and personal happiness at a young age.
- He became the pillar of a broken family, holding together a kingdom that often misunderstood him.
- He watched his grandchildren destroy one another in the Mahabharata war.
- He was **shot with arrows and lay in pain for days,** yet never cursed anyone not even those who betrayed him.

Lesson:

Many men today are like Bhishma...loyal, duty-bound but broken inside.

They are raised to protect everyone but themselves, to love without expecting love in return.

Bhishma's story is not just of sacrifice but of how neglecting one's emotional needs can lead to deep inner suffering.

To Society: A Request

A Heartfelt Request to Society- From the Heart of Author

To every parent, partner, teacher, boss and friend let us pause for a moment and ask ourselves: when was the last time we told a man its okay to cry?

When did we remind a son that his worth isn't only in his salary? When did we last listen just not to respond but to understand....a brother, a husband, a father, a friend?

Men, too, break.

Not with noise, but in silence.

They suffer in silence, hiding their war behind the smile- the weight of unspoken expectations, the pressure to provide, the fear of being seen as weak and the unbearable burden of being "strong" all the time.

This door is not just about male suicides; it is a mirror to a society that forgot to hold space for a man's pain.

And so, this is a request to you, dear reader:

- Be kinder to the men around you.
- Don't dismiss their silence as strength it might be sorrow.
- Teach your sons that being human is more important than being
- 'Tough.'

- Tell your brothers that they are allowed to feel.
- Show your fathers that even pillars deserve support.
- Tell your husbands that their value lies in their presence, not just their paycheck.

Let us not wait for another man to quietly vanish from our lives before we realize...we should have asked....we should have listened....we should have cared.....

Let's rewrite the rules.

Let's rebuild a society that doesn't just expect strength from men but offers it back when they need it most.

Because a man's life is worthy of love, support and understanding. And it must never end in silence.

A Letter to Every Man Reading This

You are not just a provider. You are a person.

You don't have to carry the world on your shoulders. You deserve love. You deserve to be understood.

You deserve to cry. Heal. & still be seen as Strong.

If you ever thought ending it all was the only way.....please wait. ***Talk to someone.***

Message a friend. Call a helpline. Write it out.

But don't let the world lose another you.

A Final Word to You;

You gave your love. You gave your loyalty.

And someone turned it into your deepest pain.

But don't let it destroy you.

Don't let betrayal define your worth.

You are not just a husband.

You are a man with a heart, a dream and a future.

You can rise again.

And you will.

The truth will always find its voice. And when it does, let it sound like your comeback....not your goodbye.

Exiting Door 6

If this door helped even one man feel seen,

If even one woman holds space for the silence he hides, if even one life is saved from choosing the end.

Then this door has spoken what words often cannot: You matter. **You are not alone.**

Key to Door 7

THIS KEY CARRIES THE COURAGE THEY WERE DENIED

DOOR 7
YOU
ARE
NOT
BROKEN

Already Broken

The Quiet Suicides of LGBTQ+ Souls

Some wounds don't bleed but burn. Every day, someone wakes up in a body they don't recognize... a voice they fear... a world that stares at them like they don't belong.

They fix their clothes in the mirror not to feel good, but to appear "normal."

They learn to walk differently, speak less, or laugh quieter not because they want to, but because *someone told them they should.*

Some are born boys but feel like girls. Some fall in love with the same gender. Some feel neither. Some feel both. And some are still figuring it out.

But most importantly **they are human. Just like you. Just like me.**

Yet the world divide. Laughs at them. Questions them. Converts them into jokes in WhatsApp groups. Or worse... silences them with prayers they never asked for.

Read This Slowly If You're One of Them

To the one reading this in secret,

To the one who cries every night, wondering if anyone will ever love them for who they are.....

To the one who's been called a sin, a shame, a mistake.....

To the one who's afraid of being disowned for simply *existing.*

Please, pause. Breathe. And know this: You are not a sin. You are a soul.

True Stories, Silenced Hearts

- **Anonymous, R,** age 20, jumped from her college building in Delhi after her classmates mocked her sexuality for months. Her last WhatsApp message to her best friend was, "Tell my parents I didn't choose this. I just chose honesty."
- **Anonymous, P**, a transgender teen from Pune, left a letter that read, "I couldn't be a good son. I wasn't allowed to be a daughter either."
- **Anonymous, H, 25,** was a brilliant painter. His parents tore apart his art and called it "gay nonsense." He overdosed on sleeping pills. No one even knew he was in pain.

These aren't headlines. These were human beings...with dreams, with love, with the same right to live freely.

What Breaks Them Before Death Does:

- When they are **forced into marriages,** knowing they'll die every day in silence.
- When they are told, *"It's just a phase."*
- When they get bullied in school, mocked in college and isolated at work.
- When their own families become strangers.
- When they have to beg to be called by the right name or pronoun. And the worst?

When they begin to believe that they are unworthy of love. That the world would be better off without them.

<u>What Can Be Done:</u> For Them, With Them, By Us For Society:

- Talk openly about LGBTQ+ identities in homes, schools and temples.
- Stop mocking, stop moral policing and stop forcing "corrections."
- Celebrate Pride not just in parades but in conversations, in hiring, in parenting.

Practical Solutions for Parents of LGBTQ+ Children:

- **Pause Judgement, Practice Listening:** Your child did not "become" this way...they were *born* this way. Don't rush into correction or denial. Just sit, breathe and listen. Say, *"Thank you for trusting me. I want to understand."* Even that one sentence can save a life.
- **Separate Fear from Love:** Many parents fear what "society will say." But your child isn't society's Child, they're *yours*.

  Don't let the fear of others become louder than the love you have for your own blood.

  Protect them even if that means protecting them from your own conditioning.
- **Educate Yourself:** Not knowing is okay. Staying ignorant is not.

  Read trusted books, articles, watch videos on gender identity & sexuality. Ask experts. Talk to parents who've walked this path.

  Learn the difference between transgender, gay, lesbian, bisexual, non- binary.
- **Use Their Name and Pronouns:** If your child tells you their preferred name or pronoun...**respect it**.

  It's not just grammar; it's dignity.

Mistakes may happen but correcting yourself each time shows you care.

- **Don't Force Silence:** Telling your child to "hide it" or "never tell anyone" Is like putting a pillow over their spirit.

  Let them be seen, Let them be real. They deserve a life, not a lie.

- **Keep the Faith, but Expand It:** Many parents struggle because of religious beliefs. But every faith teaches love and compassion.

  Search deeper. God did not ask you to stop loving your child. If you still believe they need prayers then pray for their protection, not their change.

- **Seek Support Together:** Go to family therapy or LGBTQ+ support groups together. You don't have to "fix" anything. you just need to walk beside them. This will show your child that they're not alone in the journey.

- **Say It Out Loud:** Don't just accept them silently also affirm them actively. Tell your child, "You are not broken. I am proud of you. I love you exactly as you are."

  This one sentence can undo years of shame they've carried.

- **Shield Them from Harmful Relatives:** Some relatives or neighbors may be cruel. Don't be neutral. **Be their protector.** Say, *"In this house, we don't tolerate hate. We protect our child."*

  That courage can build your child's confidence for life.

- **Remember: You are Building a Legacy of Love:** One day, when your child grows stronger and braver, they'll tell the world

  "My parents didn't give up on me. They became my safe home." Be that story.

Practical Solutions for Institutions Supporting LGBTQ+ Individuals:

- **Adopt a Zero-Tolerance Policy Against Bullying and Discrimination:** Make it crystal clear: homophobia, transphobia or any form of discrimination will not be tolerated.

  This must apply to staff, students, guests and even management. Put it in writing. Enforce it.

- **Train Your Staff with Sensitivity Programs:** Include regular workshops on gender identity, mental health and LGBTQ+ inclusion.

  Teachers, wardens, HR and healthcare providers must be sensitized.

  Most discrimination happens **not out of hate, but ignorance.** Let knowledge heal.

- **Create Safe Reporting Systems:** Allow students, employees to **report harassment anonymously**. Ensure that their identity is protected and action is taken fairly. A safe reporting space is a lifeline.

- **Respect Identity on Paper & in Practice**

  - Allow for **chosen names/ pronouns** in ID cards, email addresses, certificates.
  - Enable gender-neutral forms and paperwork.
  - This isn't just admin work it's **a declaration of dignity.**

- **Provide Gender-Neutral Facilities:** Create at least **one gender-neutral washroom** on campus or office premises. This simple change saves people from daily fear and embarrassment. It says: *We see you. We respect your safety.*

- **Make Mental Health Support LGBTQ+ Friendly:** Appoint or train counselors to be non-judgmental, aware and LGBTQ+ sensitive.

  Give students or employees access to confidential & free mental health help.

  Sometimes, just **one validating conversation** can stop a suicide.

- **Celebrate Diversity, Don't Just Tolerate It:**

  Observe Pride Month. Host open forums. Invite LGBTQ+ speakers or Changemakers.

  Normalize conversations that humanize identities. Diversity is not a challenge, it is a strength.

- **Create Support Groups on Campus or Within Workplaces:** Let LGBTQ+ students or employees connect safely with each other. Give them permission and space to form communities. This **peer support** can be life-changing.

- **Protect Trans Rights in Hiring & Promotion:** For workplaces: hiring trans or non-binary persons should not be tokenism.

  Build real, respectful spaces for their growth, safety or career development.

Final Note to Institutions:

"You may not change the world but if you change your own system, you might just save someone's child."

Psychological Healing & Support for LGBTQ+ Individuals:

Because your mind deserves the same safety your soul seeks.

1. **Identity Affirmation Exercises**
    - Speak your truth aloud daily: "I am not a mistake. I am a miracle becoming visible."
    - Use journals, audio recordings, or mirrors to affirm who you are.
    - List what makes you **unique, not wrong.**

✓ *Why it helps:* Builds **self-worth** by reinforcing identity in a world that tries to blur it.

2. **Releasing Internalized Shame: You are not what the world told you was wrong.**
    - Write a letter to your younger self forgiving them for hiding.
    - Burn it, tear it or bury it, ritually releasing shame.
    - Talk to a queer-friendly therapist who helps identify **inherited guilt.**

✓ *Why it helps:* Shame leads to silence. Releasing shame brings clarity, strength and peace.

3. **Crisis Grounding Techniques (When Feeling Suicidal or Panicked)**
    - Cold water splash or ice-cube in hand: **Pulls you back to the present.**
    - Keep an emergency note on your phone: *"You've survived everything till now. You will survive this moment too."*

✓ *Why it helps:* In panic or dysphoria episodes, the brain spins grounding brings it back.

4. **Finding Your Inner Circle**
    - Even if it's one person, have someone you can call and say:
    - *"I don't want advice....I just want to be heard."*

- Online support groups (like The Trevor Project or Indian LGBTQ+ forums) can be lifelines.
- **Chosen families** are not a concept...they are **a right.**

✅ *Why it helps:* Connection heals.

5. **Acceptance Therapy & Self-Compassion**
   - Acknowledge: "I can feel lost and still be worthy."
   - Use ACT (Acceptance & Commitment Therapy): Notice the
   - feeling → Name it → Don't resist it → Breathe through it.
   - Practice **radical self-compassion**. Say to yourself: "I am growing through something not failing at life."

✅ *Why it helps:* Fighting yourself drains life. Accepting yourself **restores it.**

6. **Therapy Modalities That Help LGBTQ+ Individuals**
   - **Narrative Therapy:** Re-write the story of your life not as tragedy but as triumph.
   - **CBT (Cognitive Behavioral Therapy):** Helps change the harmful thought patterns planted by others.
   - **Trauma-Informed Therapy:** Especially for those dealing with abuse, sexual assault, or conversion therapy.

✅ *Why it helps:* The right therapy doesn't change you...it **helps you find yourself.**

Reminder:

Healing isn't linear. Some days will hurt. Some days will feel beautiful.

You are allowed to take time. But **never give up on the masterpiece that is you.**

Legal Rights You MUST Know:

- **Section 377 Decriminalized (2018):** Homosexuality is not illegal.
- **Right to Self-Identity:** You can legally identify your gender without surgery.
- **Transgender Persons Act (2019):** Protects against discrimination in jobs, education and healthcare.
- **Right to Love & Dignity:** No one has the right to shame or harass you for your identity.

Mythological Insight:

1. Aravan & Shri Krishna (Mohini Roop)

When Prince Aravan in the Mahabharata agreed to sacrifice himself in war, he had one wish: to be married before he died. No woman came forward. Then a woman came and fulfilled his final wish with dignity & love.

Even the gods understood the importance of gender identity.

In Tamil Nadu (Villupuram district), the Koovagam festival celebrates this bond where transgender people are honored, not mocked. Ancient India accepted them. Modern India must remember that.

2. Bahuchara Mata: The Goddess of Trans Empowerment

Bahuchara Mata is worshipped in Gujarat by the Hijra community. She is a symbol of non-binary strength, courage and celibate power. Her mythology includes cursing men to become impotent if they assaulted women though she is often depicted riding a symbol of vigilance & fire. A goddess stands with those beyond the gender binary.

***Emotional Insight*:** You are not forgotten in the divine realm...**you are protected and honored.**

- *Solution*: Don't just ask for acceptance. Know that **you are already sacred.**

If this door made even one heart feel seen, one parent hug tighter, one soul believes they're not wrong for being who they are then this door has opened more than a path... it has opened hope.

You are not alone. You are not broken.

Key to Door 8

THIS KEY BREAKS FALSE CHAINS

DOOR
8
A NEW
BEGINNING

Guilty Without Proof

When Justice Becomes a Cage-
Surviving After Legal Allegations

"They freed me from jail, but never from their eyes."

What happens when a person is condemned before their guilt is proven? What becomes of the man who walks free by law but remains imprisoned by perception?

In India and across the world, there exists a silent, invisible trauma...one that isn't caused by crime but by allegation. When someone is accused, especially falsely, their identity is crushed, their relationships splinter and their soul becomes caged in fear, shame and isolation. They face a trauma worse than prison i.e social execution. Even when the courts pronounce "not guilty," society's verdict often stays the same: “He must have done something.”

Taking an Anonymous Case, a 29-year-old schoolteacher in Patna. Accused of sexual harassment by a colleague during a political vendetta, Saurabh was suspended. Despite CCTV evidence proving his innocence and a clean court verdict, the damage was irreversible. His name had already flashed across news channels. Students were told to stay away. His fiancée's family severed ties. Two years later, jobless.... Broken. He died by suicide.

His final note read: "I am free by law, but buried alive by society."

Silent Burdens That Never Fade:

Even after acquittal, these survivors carry lifelong wounds:

- **Permanent Stigma:** Society rarely distinguishes between an allegation & a conviction.
- **Professional Exclusion:** Job applications are silently discarded.

- **Media Scars:** Accusations go viral; apologies vanish in the noise.
- **Family Alienation:** Even blood relations hesitate to offer support.
- **Mental Health Collapse:** PTSD, anxiety, depression and suicidal ideation follow them like shadows.
- **Loss of Faith:** In people, in the system and often, in themselves.

Many silently ask: "How do I restart life... when the world keeps replaying my worst moment?"

Practical Solutions: For Justice to Mean Healing

1. **Legal Rights & Compensation**
   - Section 358 of IPC provides for compensation for false accusations, yet remains underutilized due to lack of awareness.
   - Legal Clean Slate Act: A proposed reform to erase the digital and legal records of acquitted individuals.
   - Fast-Track Courts: For reputation-sensitive cases, especially involving defamation, sexual harassment and public shaming.
2. **Employment Re-entry**
   - Government-assisted re-skilling programs to enable dignified employment.
   - Corporate Inclusion Incentives: Provide tax benefits to organizations that hire legally acquitted individuals.
   - Fair Employment Act: Preventing job discrimination on the basis of past allegations.
3. **Media Responsibility**
   - Ethical Reporting Bill: Mandate fair reporting of both accusation and acquittal.

- Fines and public correction campaigns for sensational/false media trials.
- Encourage independent fact-checking organizations like AltNews to be media partners in justice.

Psychological Healing: Rebuilding After False Accusations

Being falsely accused or defamed in legal proceedings based on untrue claims can be a devastating experience. The emotional toll includes shame, isolation, fear and deep psychological wounds that may linger long after the legal case is resolved. Healing in such cases requires more than just legal closure. It demands the rebuilding of identity and inner strength.

Here are key approaches that can support psychological recovery for those affected by wrongful allegations:

1. Cognitive Behavioral Therapy (CBT): Restructuring the Inner Narrative

False allegations often create deep self-doubt and internalized guilt even when a person is innocent. Over time, negative thought patterns can take root:

"What if people always believe the worst about me?" "Maybe I should have done something differently, even if I was not wrong.

CBT helps individuals recognize and challenge these distorted thoughts. It supports a shift from self-blame to self-understanding, from helplessness to empowerment. Through structured exercises, professional guidance.. survivors learn to reframe their beliefs:

"I am not defined by what was said about me.
I am defined by how I rise beyond it."

This kind of mindset work allows people to reclaim their inner dignity and begin walking the path toward emotional recovery.

2. Support Circles & Peer Empowerment

Social rejection or stigma often follows false accusations, especially in cases involving defamation or moral judgments. Many suffer in silence, fearing judgment or further scrutiny.

- **Peer-led support groups**, like *Project Second Chance*, offer a non-judgmental space where survivors can share their stories without fear. These circles validate personal truth and offer solidarity.
- **NGOs & legal support networks** can organize legal literacy camps, counseling sessions and employment support for those trying to rebuild their lives after reputational damage.

Rebuilding one's social identity is just as crucial as mental recovery. Being believed, supported and reintegrated into society is part of the healing process.

3. Creative Expression: Transforming Pain into Power

False accusations attack one's voice. Reclaiming that voice through writing, art or public speaking can be a powerful step toward psychological healing.

- **Writing workshops**, personal essays or journaling can help individuals process the emotional trauma of being misjudged or misunderstood.
- **Spoken word poetry**, podcasts or storytelling platforms allow survivors to narrate their truth and challenge public perception.
- **Art, music and theater** can serve as emotional outlets that bypass the limits of verbal expression, releasing suppressed pain in constructive ways.

By turning pain into creativity, survivors not only heal themselves but also help others understand the emotional damage false allegations can cause.

4. Inner Child Work & Reparenting: Healing from Within

False accusations can reopen old wounds especially for those who were judged, silenced or misunderstood in childhood. Inner child work addresses the emotional residue of early neglect or injustice also it helps individuals build inner strength.

This healing method teaches survivors to:

- Care for the parts of themselves that feel afraid or shamed.
- Cultivate self-trust and emotional safety from within.
- Separate their self-worth from external judgments or social rejection.

"You were not wrong. What happened to you was."

This core affirmation helps individuals shift their perspective from internalizing blame to embracing self-compassion.

5. Restoring Identity and Self-Respect

One of the greatest damages caused by defamation or false charges is the erosion of self-respect. It can feel as though your name, reputation and truth have been stolen.

Psychological healing must involve reclaiming one's identity personally, socially infact professionally majorly:

- Reconnecting with your purpose... values.
- Engaging in meaningful work or volunteering.
- Surrounding yourself with people who see your truth and not the rumor.

Every step toward self-reclamation is a step away from shame and toward dignity.

My Dear Reader Always Remember:

False allegations can fracture lives but they do not have to define them. With the right psychological tools, support systems, inner work, individuals; can not only survive such injustice but emerge stronger and more grounded.

In the journey towards *Suicide Mukt Bharat*, we must include those who have been wrongly accused or defamed. Their emotional pain is real and their healing deserves recognition and support.....not further silence.

Society's Role: The Second Trial

When a person is accused rightly or wrongly their first trial takes place in a courtroom. But too often, the **second trial begins outside** in our streets, homes, workplaces and whispers. This second trial is not governed by law. It is governed by stigma. And unlike the first, it offers no lawyers, no evidence nothing...indeed no chance at justice.

This is the silent punishment society inflicts on those who have already suffered enough. A punishment that lingers far beyond any legal sentence. It is time we recognize our role in this invisible sentence and change it.

We must stop being the second judge.

When we label and isolate people who've been accused or imprisoned often without knowing the full truth, we strip them of their dignity and mostly their right to rebuild.

We must ask ourselves: **Are we healing people, or permanently breaking them?**

1. Family Education Programs: Healing Must Begin at Home

The first space a person returns to after legal battles is their home. Yet, this space is often filled with emotional distance.

- Families need structured **education programs** that address how to support a loved one after false allegations or defamation.
- Healing conversations, emotional literacy and guided counseling can help families move from **"What will people say?"** to **"We are with you."**

Home should be a shelter not another courtroom. When families stand beside the accused with love and trust, they help restore not just one person, but a broken system.

2. Empathy Curriculum: Teaching Justice Beyond the Law

What if we raised a generation that doesn't rush to judgment? What if students learned not just dates and laws but the human cost of injustice?

- **Empathy-driven education** should be embedded in school curriculums. Case studies of wrongful accusations, prison reform and restorative justice must be included not as legal content, but as human stories.
- Let young minds explore not only **what is right**, but **what is kind.** Not just **who is guilty**, but **who is hurting.**

When we teach children to ask, *"What if it were me?"* we begin shaping a society rooted in compassion, not condemnation.

3. Community Rehabilitation Hubs: Giving Lives a Second Chance

Rebuilding life after false allegations is one of the hardest journeys a person can undertake. The world may move on, but the survivor often remains frozen unemployable and ofcourse unheard.

- Community Rehabilitation Hubs should exist in every district not just for legal aid, but for emotional healing, job placement, therapy and reintegration.
- These hubs must be safe spaces, where survivors can share without shame, learn new skills and connect with mentors who believe in their potential.

Offering someone a job, a chance to speak or simply a seat at the table can be the difference between suicide and survival.

To Build Suicide Mukt Bharat:

We often say "justice must be served," but forget that **mercy must be practiced.**

In our mission toward a *Suicide Mukt Bharat,* it's not enough to focus on law reform, mental health or crisis response. We must go deeper. We must unlearn cruelty disguised as culture. We must question gossip disguised as truth. We must stop turning our backs on those who are trying to rise again.

Because when a person is denied a second chance by society, **they are not just being punished....they are being erased.**

Let us not be the reason someone gives up on life. Let us be the reason someone chooses to live again

Existing Government & Institutional Support for Ex-Convicts in India:

1. Vocational Training and Skill Development in Prisons

Across many Indian states, prison departments have introduced vocational training programs aimed at preparing inmates for employment after release. These include training in tailoring, carpentry, food production, electrical repair.

For example, prisons in Odisha, Kerala, Delhi and Maharashtra operate structured workshops and skill programs in partnership with institutions like the National Institute of Open Schooling (NIOS) or Indira Gandhi National Open University (IGNOU). Upon release, many trained individuals are better equipped to find work or start small businesses.

In some correctional institutions like Tihar Jail in Delhi, products made by inmates are sold under brand names like "TJ's," creating a sense of purpose and self-worth.

2. Financial Assistance & Seed Grants

In certain states, the government has initiated financial support schemes specifically for ex-convicts. Kerala runs a rehabilitation program that offers a one-time grant of ₹10,000 to individuals from below-poverty-line (BPL) families after release, with the aim of helping them start a small trade or business.

Similarly, the Assam government has provided financial aid to released life convicts from underprivileged backgrounds to encourage economic self-reliance.

These efforts recognize that financial hardship is one of the major barriers to lawful reintegration and must be addressed early.

3. Prison Industries & Public/Private Partnerships

Several prison systems across India have partnered with private companies and social enterprises to create in-prison industries. These include weaving units, packaging units, bakery operations and even automotive component assembly lines.

Such models are found in Rajasthan, Goa, Tamil Nadu and Madhya Pradesh, where prisons collaborate with firms to teach inmates transferable job skills. These programs offer practical training, modest income and a work ethic that continues to benefit them post-release.

4. Counseling, Education & Emotional Support

Mental health and education are integral to rehabilitation. Many prisons offer basic education, vocational diplomas, access to counseling or wellness programs. Meditation, yoga, art therapy, music etc. are being used in states like Delhi & Karnataka as tools for self-reflection and inner healing.

NGOs such as India Vision Foundation and Prayas Foundation work alongside government institutions to support ex-inmates through counseling or family reunification services.

5. After-Care and Probation Services

Most states operate probation services under their Social Welfare Departments. In places like Kerala...Assam, probation officers assist with legal follow-up, counseling and help individuals connect with employment schemes or educational opportunities.

Some states also run After-Care Homes or community-based support initiatives for former inmates who have no family support, especially youth or women who are more vulnerable post-release.

Humble Request of Author to Dignitaries/ Government: From Verdict to Restoration

The government's role shouldn't end with delivering justice in court. True justice extends beyond the verdict. When individuals re-enter society and work to rebuild their lives. For those who have been acquitted a sentence, the greatest challenge often isn't the legal process but starting fresh in a world that still views them through the lens of their past.

To ensure they are not pushed into isolation or hopelessness, it is essential that the government actively supports their reintegration not just through laws, but through structured opportunities. Few Ideas that can take place:

- **Punarjanam Scheme: A New Beginning Under Skill India**

I request to propose the launch of **Punarjanam Scheme**, a targeted government program under the **Skill India Mission**, designed to support people who have been legally cleared or released from custody.

The program would offer:

- o **Professional training and job placement support** to help individuals re-enter the workforce with dignity.
- o **Access to mental health and career counseling**, especially for those impacted by long legal proceedings.
- o **Dedicated support centers** where individuals can update records, apply for loans and receive legal guidance on reintegration.

The goal is simple: to help individuals return to life not as ex-accused or ex-convicts but as citizens with potential.

- **Judicial Review Panels: Learning from Wrongful Cases**

In many cases, people are exculpating after years of legal battles. But there are rarely any follow-up by the system. False cases are treated as closed chapters without looking into the damage caused or how to prevent future misuse.

I with full gratitude request the formation of **Judicial Review Panels** at the state and national levels. These panels should:

- Identify patterns in wrongful or exaggerated accusations, especially in sensitive cases.
- Recommend reforms to prevent misuse of laws.
- Issue formal exoneration letters that individuals can use to clear their name in official records and background checks.

Also, Updating Identity Records: Role of NCRB and UIDAI- Even after an acquittal, old charges sometimes continue to show up in background checks, digital ID systems or verification databases. This can prevent individuals from applying for jobs, traveling or even renting a house.

Restoring someone's digital and official identity is not just a technical necessity.....it's a matter of basic justice.

The State must stand not only as an authority but also as a support system. Those who are cleared by the court or have paid their debt to society deserve a fair chance to begin again.

Support is not about sympathy...it's about restoring balance. It's about removing the barriers that prevent a person from moving forward.

Government action in this space sends a powerful message: Justice is not only about punishment....it is also about making repair possible.

Mythological Insight:

Ahalya: The Woman Who Was Judged Too Soon

Ahalya. A name that should have been remembered only for grace, devotion and inner strength. But fate played its cruelest trick on her and society, as it often does so chose judgment over understanding.

Deceived by Indra, the king of gods himself "Ahalya became a victim of divine impersonation". Her only "mistake" was not seeing through a disguise. And for that, she was cursed, turned to stone silenced, shamed and forgotten. Her truth buried beneath the weight of an accusation she could not even explain.

For years, she lay still. Not just in body, but in the eyes of the world. No one came to ask her story. No one came to say: "We believe you."

But **Shri Ram** came.

The *Maryada Purushottam*, the upholder of truth, the one who stood for righteousness. He came not to judge, but to save. With his divine wisdom, he understood what others had failed to see that Ahalya was **not guilty**, only **wronged**.

He did not ask for proof.

He did not doubt her silence.

He simply touched the stone...with that one act, gave her back her life and her dignity.

And the world took note. If **Ram**, the most righteous of all, did not judge her, then who were we to doubt her?

From that day onward, **Ahalya was no longer remembered as cursed.** She became a symbol of **purity and restored honor.**

Lesson: If the greatest protector of dharma could offer Ahalya acceptance without interrogation then why can't we?

Why do we, in today's world, become so quick to shame someone accused? Why do we forget that justice isn't only a verdict. It is also the **opportunity to return.**

If our **judiciary,** our **police** and our **respectful voices in society** take a stand

if they say, *"This person must not be destroyed by false allegations"* then slowly but surely, the healing begins...Dignity returns... Life reopens!!

And most importantly, that person who once stood on the edge, haunted by suicidal thoughts finds hope again. They remember who they were before the labels. They breathe without fear. They live again not in hiding, but with their head held high.

A Letter to Bring You Back to Yourself"

Dear You,

If you're reading this with heavy eyes and heavier heart If you've been lying awake at night wondering, "How did things come to this?"

If you're tired of pretending you're okay while you're breaking inside... then this letter is for you.

I don't need to know every detail of your situation to understand one thing clearly: You're hurting more than anyone knows.

Maybe you've been blamed for something you didn't do. Maybe you've faced judgment, rejection, silence or even hatred and I am sure none of it was your fault.

And now, you're left wondering whether continuing to live like this is even worth it.

But before you go further down that road of thoughts that feel too dark.

I want to tell you something that no one else may have said out loud:

Don't leave. Not like this. Not when your story isn't finished yet.

Whatever has happened to you ***it doesn't define you.***

You are not what people say. You are not what a moment in time tried to make you believe.

You are still you. Still valuable. Still needed. And please ***don't leave your family behind.*** *They may not have known what to say.*

They may have made mistakes.

But this was never their fault either. They love you in ways they don't

always show.

They deserve to see you smile again. ***you deserve to feel peace again.***

And if you're someone who says, "I don't have anyone" then please believe this from me:

The world is not empty. There are still good people waiting to meet you.

People who will believe in you.

People who will listen.

People who will call you by your name, not by your past. But first you have to stay.

You have to fight through this one more day and then another. Not to prove anything to anyone.

But to give yourself the life you still deserve.

Start small. Join someone. Talk. Sit in a room where you're heard.

If there's no one around...... ***reach out to me.***

I'm not just an author.

I'm someone who genuinely wants you to stay alive and find reasons to smile again.

You don't need to be perfect. You just need to be here.

And I promise things will change.

With respect, with understanding and with a heart that truly cares.

Your Author

Anna

Final Impact Statement:

As you walk out of this DOOR, don't just walk....rise. Walk with such confidence, such calm strength, that people around you stop and say, "Is this a rebirth?"

Just like Lord Krishna, who was born in a jail but when he stepped out, the whole world felt a powerful energy. He didn't let the darkness of his birth stop him. He lived with such wisdom, such love and such strength, that even today the world learns from his words.

Let this be your moment too. Forget what happened in the past. Don't worry about what the future will bring. Focus only on this moment **this life, right now.**

And live it in such a beautiful way, that people look at you and feel inspired. Let them say, "This person didn't give up. This person came back stronger."

Live in a way that your pain turns into someone else's hope. Live in a way that your journey becomes someone else's reason to hold on.

Because you didn't just survive... you were born again with a purpose.

Key to Door 9

THIS KEY HONORS YOUR INVISIBLE BATTLES

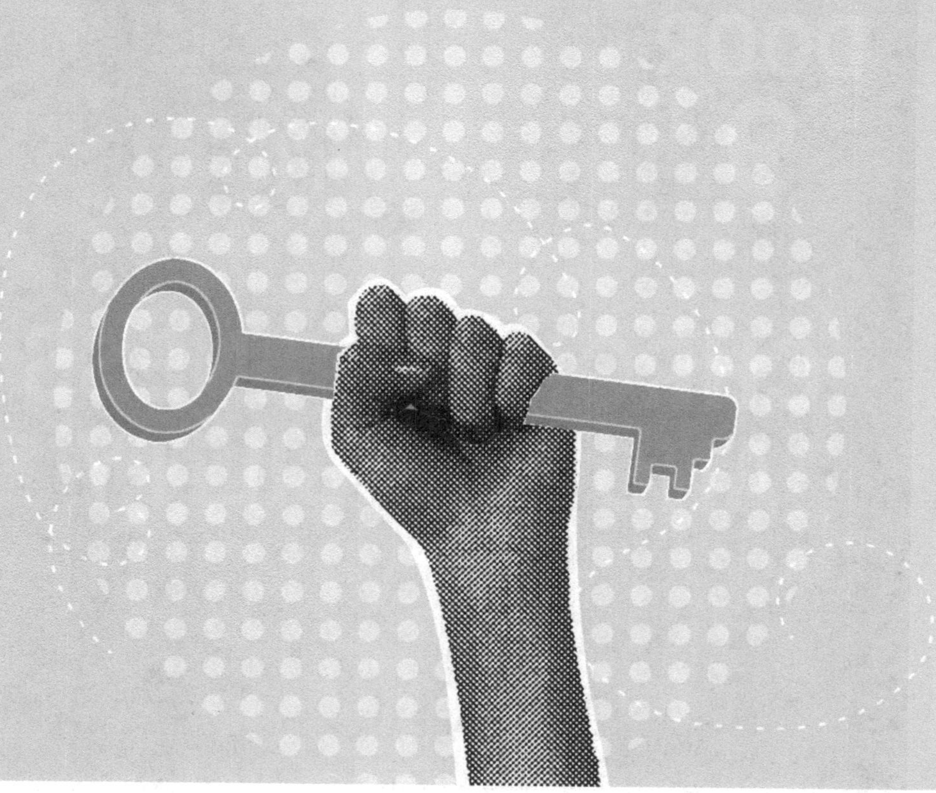

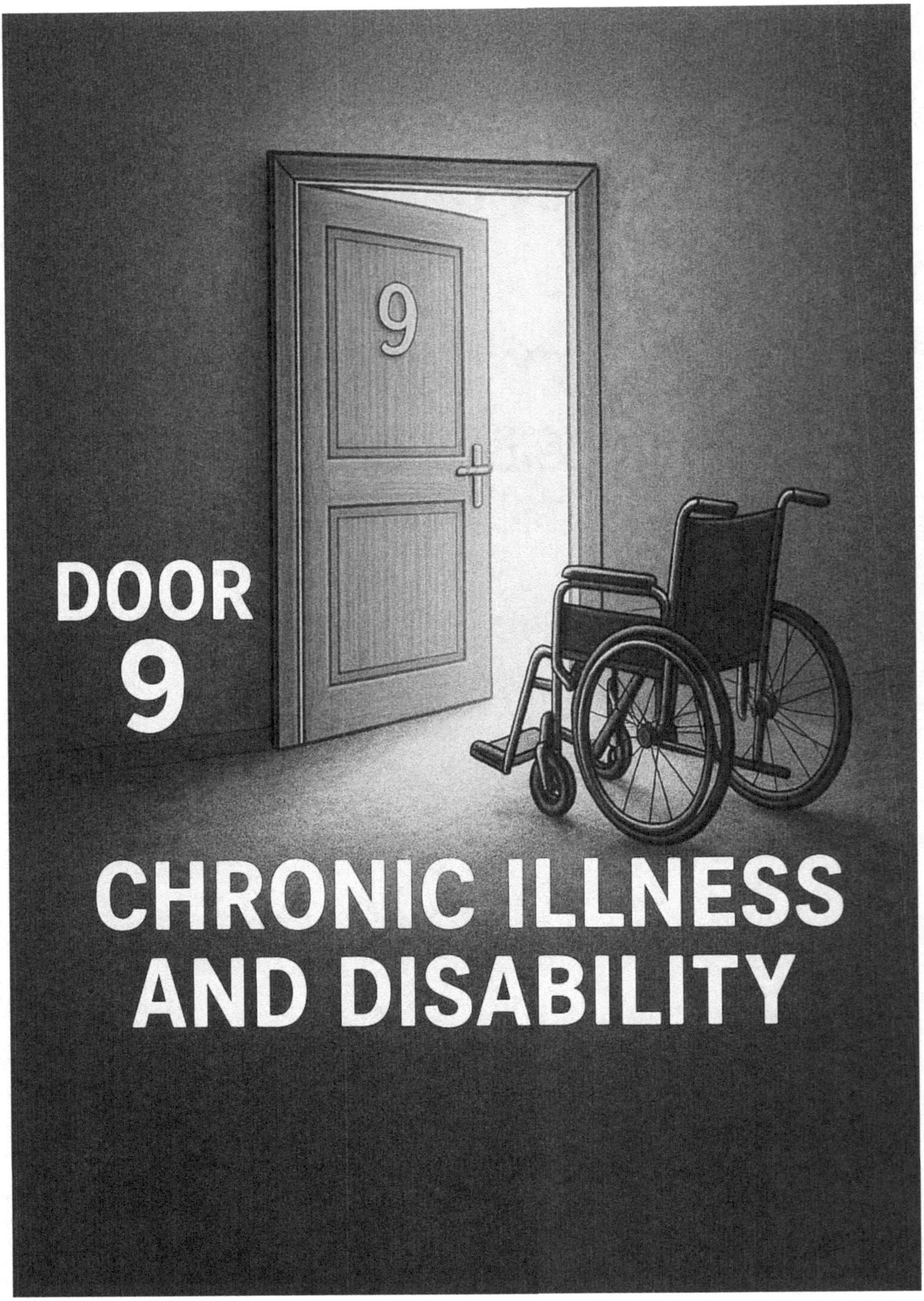
9
DOOR
9
CHRONIC ILLNESS
AND DISABILITY

Illness Took Over

Suicide Due to Chronic Illness & Disability

The Silent Scream Behind the Smile:

Every year, over **13,000** people in India die by suicide due to chronic illness and physical disability, according to NCRB data. But these numbers barely capture the silent, invisible suffering behind closed doors the sigh that never becomes a cry, the pain that never finds a name.

Across India and the world, millions endure **chronic illnesses**; say, cancer, autoimmune diseases, kidney or heart failure, diabetes, neurological disorders and countless others live with **permanent physical disabilities** due to birth conditions, accidents, or progressive diseases. But what truly breaks them isn't the diagnosis it's the life that changes after it.

When your body becomes a battlefield, your soul often becomes the casualty. Friends start fading. Invitations stop coming. Even your reflection begins to look like a stranger.

Every morning becomes a fight to rise. Every night becomes a test of endurance.

You feel like a burden.

You begin to wonder: *"If my body won't heal, what's the point of staying?"*

This is the pain we must speak of not to pity but to understand. Because behind every tearless eye is a soul aching to be seen not as a patient or disabled person but as a human who once had dreams and desire.

A Truth That Hurts: Why Do They Choose Death?

- **Isolation:** Illness traps them in beds and behind closed doors. Loneliness becomes louder than pain.
- **Loss of Identity:** The athlete who can't run anymore. The singer who loses their voice. The woman who once danced and now can't move without support.
- **Financial Drain:** Expensive treatments, lifelong medications, constant travel to hospitals. The guilt of 'ruining' their family's savings.
- **Emotional Dependence:** Asking someone to help you to the toilet chips away at your dignity, day by day.
- **Societal Labels:** "Bechara", "burden", "useless". Words spoken casually by others can become invisible nooses.
- **Endless Pain**: Physical agony, fatigue and sleepless nights can push even the strongest minds toward darkness.

They don't die because they are weak. They die because they feel forgotten. They don't want death they just want the pain, the pity, the prison... to end.

Real-Life Echoes of Pain:

Heartfelt Story of my brother Abhishek Kumar: There is a boy whose eyes were once the most beautiful thing about him. He was lovingly called as "Happy." But at the tender age of 24, he began to lose his vision completely. Today, he lives in darkness, unable to see the world he once admired so deeply.

But here's what makes his story unforgettable: **he never gave up**.

He laughs. He listens to music. He helps others. He love his kids a lot. He chooses life. And even though the world cannot imagine the silent grief of losing sight, he has become a light for many. His **willpower** and his **quiet strength** continue to inspire everyone around him.

And over time, he turned deeply spiritual. He began to meditate, chant and find stillness within. His connection with the divine became so strong that it became the secret to his **happiness**, his **peace** and his **courage**.

He may have lost his vision but he never lost his vision for life. His soul now sees what the eyes never could.

Anonymous Story - A: A 16-year-old boy who lost both legs in a train accident said, "The stares outside hurt more than the train did." He now paints with his mouth, but he still fights suicidal thoughts on quiet nights.

These are not rare tragedies. They are silent realities.

Practical & Medical Solutions:

1. **Mental Health Access**

   - Offer **free, regular therapy** in all government and private hospitals for patients battling long-term or life-threatening illnesses. Mental suffering is just as critical as physical pain and both deserve equal treatment.
   - Make **psychological support mandatory** during extended hospital stays, cancer treatments, dialysis or disability rehabilitation.
   - Provide **emotional intelligence training** for caregivers and family members. A kind word, a warm hug or a patient ear can sometimes heal more than any injection.

When someone is going through a storm inside their body, they need shelter for their mind too.

2. **Job Opportunities for the Disabled**

   - Create dedicated **work-from-home job portals** for people with chronic illnesses and limited mobility, matching them with meaningful employment that respects their conditions.
   - Enforce **diversity hiring quotas** not as a token gesture but as a celebration of all human ability.

- Start **vocational retraining programs** designed with love and dignity helping every individual find a role where their strength is valued and their condition is respected.

Give them not sympathy, but a salary. Not charity but a chance.

3. **Financial & Medical Aid**

- **Increase disability pensions** so that surviving each month doesn't
- feel like begging for breath.
- **Subsidize essential assistive devices** like wheelchairs, catheters, home-care beds, adult diapers and hearing aids. These are not luxuries they are lifelines.
- Provide **tax exemptions and financial benefits** to families who care for someone severely ill or disabled, because their everyday life is often full of invisible sacrifices.

When disease drains the body, finances should not break the spirit.

4. **Community Networks:** Encourage every school, college, society and neighborhood to "adopt" a disabled person or chronic patient. This is not about donation it's about compassion through connection. A weekly visit, a shared meal, a phone call these tiny acts can breathe life back into someone.

   Organize Disability Pride Weeks not as a formality, but as a reminder to society that strength wears many forms.

   Launch home visit campaigns by local volunteers, doctors or students for those who can't travel so they know they are still seen, still loved and still remembered.

A Special Word to Hospital Nurses, Staff & NGO Warriors:

To all the **nurses, hospital attendants, rehabilitation center staff, NGO volunteers** and **caregivers** reading this. You are the unseen angels who hold trembling hands, change bedsheets soaked in tears and lift bodies that have forgotten how to stand.

But I know it's not easy. I know it's tiring.

The tantrums, the pain, the endless calls for help... it's more than just a job.

It's emotional labor.

But please, please...

Be patient. Be kind. Be gentle.

Because sometimes, your behavior becomes the deciding moment in someone's will to live.

The way you speak, the way you pause, the way you smile... may feel small to you but to them, it's everything.

It could be the one reason they choose to **live another day.**

You are not just treating a patient.

You are **touching a soul** that is already scared, already hurting, already halfway into darkness.

Psychological Healing: Restoring the Light Within

- **CBT and Mindfulness**: Sometimes, the illness doesn't just attack the body it creeps into the soul. Cognitive Behavioral Therapy helps untangle those lies: *"I am broken"* ,*"I am worthless."*

  With mindfulness, we teach the mind to pause and to breathe:

  "You are not your pain. You are not your diagnosis. You are still YOU."

- **Art and Music Therapy:** When words fail, colors speak. When silence hurts, melodies heal.

  A paintbrush, a drumbeat, a dance...these are not hobbies. They are survival tools.

They allow the pain to flow without shame and the heart to speak without fear.

- **Pet Therapy:** Sometimes, healing arrives on four legs with a wagging tail. Animals don't see wheelchairs, scars or oxygen tanks. They see love and give it endlessly. Their presence reminds us that we're not alone. That joy is still possible even in brokenness.

- **Faith Counseling:** Not to preach. Not to convert. But to comfort the spirit.

  When medicine stops working, sometimes faith steps in.

  In silent praying many find peace. Some rediscover God. Others discover themselves.

- **Support Groups:** There's unmatched magic in hearing, "*Me too.*"

  A circle of people, all carrying invisible burdens, holding space for one another. No masks. No judgments.

  Just real stories, real struggles and a powerful reminder: "You may feel alone, but you never truly are."

Society's Role: From Spectator to Supporter

- **Stop staring. Start speaking:** That one long glance from you might feel like a passing second...

  But to the person in the wheelchair, or the one walking with a limp, or the one wearing a catheter bag it can feel like a lifetime of judgment.

  Look into their eyes not their wounds. Speak with warmth, not silence.

  Because silence often screams louder than words.

- **Stop pitying. Start participating:** Pity is a cage that isolates. It makes them feel like an "other."

What they need isn't your sorrow your time and your presence. Sit beside them. Laugh with them. Cry if you have to but let them feel human again, not a problem to be solved.

- **Stop sidelining. Start including:** Every time you say, "Let's not call them, it'll be awkward," a heart breaks somewhere.

  Include them not as an act of kindness, but because they deserve joy, stories, laughter and belonging.

  Pull out a chair at your table. Send that wedding invite. Celebrate their birthdays.

  Even one gesture of inclusion can become a memory they hold onto during their hardest nights.

Ask them, "How are *you* today?" Not "How is your condition?" Their illness is only a chapter not their entire book. Let them speak about their dreams, their hobbies and their favorite songs. Let them feel normal, if just for a moment.

Don't be afraid to touch them, hug them and hold their hand. Illness

isn't contagious until warned by the doctor.

Let your children play with theirs. Let your parents visit them. Let your life become a safe space where no one has to wear a mask of strength just to be accepted.

Let's teach every child that **real strength doesn't always roar** sometimes, it lies in the eyes of those who silently endure and still offer a smile.

Let's build a world where no one feels invisible just because their body changed.

Where no one is whispered about because they move differently. Where no soul is left out of a prayer, a party or a photograph because of how they look, walk, or speak.

Let's not just be society. Let's be a family.

Because sometimes, the difference between life and suicide... Is one friend who said, "You still matter to me."

I know there are many people who, even today, **hesitate to sit beside or speak with those who are mentally challenged, chronically ill or physically disabled.** They avoid making eye contact. They skip inviting them to celebrations. They can't spare even five minutes to ask, "How are you really doing?"

Some laugh behind closed doors. Some whisper unkind things.

And some just act like they don't exist.

But please... I request you from the bottom of my heart.

Don't become that kind of human being.

Don't let your coldness or ignorance become the reason someone lies in bed at night **crying silently,** wondering why they were ever born. Don't be the reason someone says,

"It would've been better if I was dead."

I make this humble request to every reader holding this book in their hands:

Take out a few minutes from your life... just a few... To sit with someone who's suffering.

Not just at an NGO or a hospital or a community drive, But in your own home.

Your own neighborhood. Your own workplace.

Maybe there's an old grandfather in your house who no longer feels seen.

Maybe there's a grandmother who walks slowly, whose hands tremble, who smiles but hides pain.

Sit with them. Hold their hand. Let them speak. Don't rush. Don't interrupt.

Maybe there's a colleague in your office who doesn't speak, but hears everything...feels everything.

Maybe they walk differently. Maybe they eat slowly.

But they, too, deserve to be included. To be spoken to with kindness.

Please, don't be that person who becomes **a reason for someone's desire to die.**

Be someone's reason to hold on.

Be the light they see when everything else around them feels dark.

God has given you a body that works, a mind that functions and a life full of ability.

Be thankful not just with words, but with actions.

Use your strength to lift someone else.

Use your voice to speak life into someone else's silence. Use your time to make someone feel like they still belong.

Remember, it takes **just five minutes** to sit beside someone, smile at them, ask about their day and say: *"You still matter. You are not forgotten."*

Sometimes, those five minutes can save a life. Because in this world full of noise and neglect...

Your compassion might be the only medicine someone ever receives.

Government Intervention: From Policy to Practice

- Extend **Ayushman Bharat** to cover rare and long-term illnesses.
- Make the **UDID card** universal and usable across all services.
- Offer **direct cash transfers** and insurance for palliative care.
- Start **Disability Well-being Indexes** for states.
- Helplines specifically for the emotionally struggling disabled.

Mythological Insight: The Sacred Power in Imperfection

When Sage **Ashtavakra** entered King Janak's court, many laughed at his deformed body. But when he spoke, the entire court stood in silence. Wisdom poured from a twisted frame. Truth echoed from a crooked spine.

When **Shabari,** an old tribal woman with hunched shoulders and torn feet, waited years for Lord Ram, he came to her first not for her offerings but her love.

Disability in our mythology never meant weakness. It meant divinity. Their light was too bright to be hidden in flesh.

Living Inspirations:

A Ray of Light: The Story of Arunima Sinha

There are moments in life when tragedy knocks without warning. One such moment came for Arunima Sinha, a national-level volleyball player, who never imagined that a single train journey would change her life forever and yet, it did.

In 2011, while traveling to Delhi, Arunima was pushed from a moving train by robbers when she resisted their attempt to snatch her bag and gold chain. She landed on the adjacent railway track. In the split of a second, another train came roaring from the opposite side and in a horrifying turn of fate, she lost her left leg.

Can we imagine that pain? A young girl in her early twenties, filled with dreams and talent, lying on a railway track broken and abandoned.

She was not just physically shattered, but emotionally torn. For any ordinary soul this could have been the end. For many, this level of trauma, pain and disability becomes a reason to give up on life. It could have been easier for her to sink into darkness, to feel hopeless, to question "Why me?"

But Arunima chose something else. She chose life. She chose to create meaning from her pain.

While lying in the hospital, barely out of danger she made a decision that stunned everyone:

"I will climb Mount Everest."

People laughed. Doctors were concerned. Family members were in disbelief. But Arunima had made a silent pact with herself. Not only would she rise again, she would rise so high that the world would look up to her.

With a prosthetic leg, enduring physical pain, emotional trauma and thousands of hurdles, she trained herself in mountaineering. She was guided and mentored by none other than Bachendri Pal, the first Indian woman to climb Everest.

And in May 2013, Arunima created history.

She became the world's first female amputee to scale Mount Everest.

The same girl who lay helpless on the tracks... stood proud on the roof of the world. This is not a fairytale it's a true story its someone's life biggest truth (Sourced from wikipedia).

Why This Story Matters in the Battle Against Suicide:

For those struggling with chronic illness, disability or sudden physical loss, the emotional trauma can often feel heavier than the body itself. The world becomes unfamiliar. Dreams feel far away. One's own body seems like a prison.

But Arunima's story reminds us:

"You are not your pain. You are what you do with your pain."

She didn't allow her amputation to amputate her dreams.

She didn't let disability become her identity.

She turned her pain into her power, her tears into triumph.

In moments when your body betrays you or illness shakes your very identity remember Arunima. When life feels unfair and cruel...remember that your spirit is stronger than your suffering.

A Mythological Reflection:

In our scriptures, even Lord Shiva drank poison during the Samudra Manthan to save the world. He turned blue "Neelkanth" bearing pain for the greater good.

Similarly, those who carry their illness and disability not as burdens, but as tools for transformation, become warriors of light in this world. Arunima Sinha, drank her share of sorrowonly to become a beacon of hope for millions.

A Letter to the One in Pain:

A Note from Me to You: As a Human, As a mother, As a Survivor

There are moments in life that break us... not with sound, but with silence. Moments that no one sees, but they live inside us haunting, hurting and shaping who we become.

This note is not written by an author. It is written by a woman who has seen pain up close. And this is not just a line...it is my truth.

For years, I silently struggled with PCOS. During some of my toughest times, I would wake up in the middle of the night and see the image of a spider...vivid, dark and terrifying. I later learned it was called a hypnopompic hallucination, a stress-induced response... but back then, it felt like my mind was turning against me.

It may sound small. But it was real. And it left me paralyzed with fear. What helped me survive was this:

Every time I commanded that image, every time I spoke back with strength.

"You are not real. You are just a thought. You don't control me."

I saw it begin to ***shrink****, to* ***fade****.*

And in that very moment, I understood the true meaning of ***self-belief****. What it feels like to take control of your mind... and win.*

That moment taught me: When you command your brain, even fear begins to dissolve.

As a woman, the most painful words I ever heard came from doctors:

"You may never become a mother."

My ***AMH levels were below 1****.... nearly every expert gave up on me. But I didn't.*

I prayed to the universe, to God and to the very cells in my body.

I changed my lifestyle. I walked the path of faith. Even I started drinking Moon Water.

And soon got blessed, I became a mother... ***not once, but twice****.*

Even during my second delivery, I remember lying on that hospital bed, whispering to myself:

"Maybe... this is it. Maybe I won't survive this time."

But I did. Because God sent me not just strength... but people who cared. My family, the nurses, the staff they carried me in ways I cannot forget.

Except one.

There was a nurse who saw my wounds and ***walked away****. She was too scared to touch me. She turned her face and left. That moment didn't just hurt, it broke something in me.*

And I realized something so painfully true:

In that moment, I wasn't just bleeding from my body... I was bleeding from the soul.

When someone sees your suffering and chooses not to care it scares you forever.

After childbirth, I suffered from ***severe anemia, postpartum depression****, intense* ***body pain*** *and* ***emotional breakdowns****.*

There were days I couldn't even walk properly. My skin broke down.

My body changed completely.

And yes ***people body-shamed me****, unaware that I was already drowning on the inside.*

But pain didn't stop there.

Even today... some people still try to make me feel ***"less than."***

Not for my actions. Not for my values.

But for something I never chose ***my skin colour.***

My husband has a fairer complexion and I have a wheatish skin tone and of course, after having two children, some changes in appearance are inevitable.

But what's more difficult than the physical changes are ***dealing with the comparisons that follow.***

And people sometimes even unknowingly compare me with him, with their eyes, with their words.

What hurts the most is when they ***compare my own children's skin tone to mine****, saying,*

"Oh, the kids are fair like their father...not like the mother."

Imagine... your own children being praised in a way that indirectly ***puts down their own mother.***

Yes, my husband has always been supportive, but I won't lie. There have been times when these ***subtle discriminations****, these* ***taunts wrapped in compliments****, deeply affected me.*

But not anymore.

Because today, I've educated myself.

I've trained my mind to see through the ignorance.

I've realized that ***my behavior, my kindness, my vision and my truth*** *are far greater than anyone's biased opinion.*

I've learned self-control. I've gained inner strength. And most importantly I've learned to smile in the face of judgment.

Just like ***Shri Krishna,*** *who responded to every taunt and every shameful label* ***not with anger but with a smile.***

That smile became his answer. That grace became his power.

And so, I remind myself if Krishna could walk through insults with a smile, so can I.

Because your soul's worth is never measured by the world's opinion.

Now when I look back at all my struggles from hormonal imbalances to hallucinations, from body shaming to childbirth complications. I realize something deeply humbling:

My problems are far smaller than those faced by people battling chronic illness or living with lifelong disability.

But there is one thing that connects us all whether it's a wound on the body or the soul:

In pain, every heart seeks care... not judgment.

So please, my dear readers if you cannot help someone, at least do not hurt them.

If you cannot praise, at least ***do not humiliate.***

If you cannot sit beside them, at least ***don't turn your face away.***

Because sometimes, all a person needs is one kind word to choose life over silence.

With every page of this book, I offer you my truth not as an expert, not as a preacher, but as human, as a ***mother*** *and as a* ***soul who chose to stand back up so she could help others rise too.***

If I can do it, so can you.

With all my love, ANNA

(A daughter of pain. A disciple of hope. A believer in new beginnings).

As you step out of Door 9, don't carry pity...carry purpose. Because your life, your story, your very breath is a part of the bigger dream i.e **Suicide Mukt Bharat,** where no one ends their life because of illness, disability or loneliness.

So, walk out not as someone who just read another chapter,

but as someone reborn with strength and with a promise to live, to let live and to remind every soul in pain:

“**You matter. You are not alone.** And your tomorrow is still waiting.”

Key to Door 10

THIS KEY UNLOCKS A FUTURE YOUR SOUL DESERVED

DOOR 10
HOPE

The Last Crop

The Farmer's Fight for Life:
Solutions Rooted in Soil, Science & Soul"

In the land of India where the farmer is worshipped as *Annadata* (the food-giver) thousands die silently every year, crushed not just by debt or drought but by neglect and helplessness.

According to the **National Crime Records Bureau (NCRB), over 10,800 farmers and agricultural labourers** died by suicide in 2023 alone. That means every hour, at least one **Annadata** gave up on life.

They die not because they're weak. They die because:

- The skies failed them.
- The banks choked them.
- The government forgot them.
- And society... society looked away.

Understanding the Farmer's Journey: A Life of Quiet Sacrifice

A farmer wakes before dawn. The world is asleep, but he's already outside

planting, watering and praying. His entire life depends on the sky, the soil, and the strength in his body. One bad monsoon and everything falls apart the crop, the income, the food on his family's plate.

And yet, **he doesn't complain.** He works harder.

But slowly, he stops smiling. He starts skipping meals so his children can eat. He worries about loans. His health suffers. He feels like a failure. And one day, when the burden becomes too much, he chooses death not because he wants to die, but because **he no longer knows how to live.**

This is not a story of one farmer. It is the story of **thousands across India.**

Men and women who feed us, yet feel they have no one to turn to.

Real Lives. Real Pain. Real Loss.

An anonymous 19-year-old girl in Telangana drank pesticide when she found her father hanging in the shed. He had borrowed money from three places for her marriage. The society whispered, "He was irresponsible." But no one paid his interest bill.

An anonymous Man, age 43, from Punjab, had over 6 acres of land. A good farmer. A proud man. But three years of failing yields and relentless pressure from private lenders, made him take poison while sitting near his tube well. His children now work as daily wage labourers.

The Root Causes: It's Not Just About Money

Many people think farmers take their lives because they are poor. But poverty is only one part of the puzzle. The truth is far more layered and heartbreaking.

Key causes include:

- Crop failure due to droughts, floods, or pests
- Heavy debts from private moneylenders with high interest
- Inability to pay for children's education or family's medical needs
- Delayed or denied government aid and crop insurance
- Lack of access to fair markets and fair prices
- Shame, guilt and a sense of helplessness
- No mental health support
- Social stigma especially among male farmers who are expected to "stay strong"

Behind every suicide is a story of **unmet needs & unseen tears.**

Practical & Scientific Solutions: That Can Save Lives

Solving farmer suicides needs more than sympathy. It needs **strong systems, sensitive people** and **sustainable policies.**

Here are **12 solutions** that combine **heart and science:**

1. Rural Mental Health Volunteers

Train ASHA workers or local volunteers to recognize signs of depression or suicidal thoughts. Offer **basic counseling, emotional support and referrals** to experts.

Why? Because one conversation can save a life.

2. 24x7 Farmer Helplines with Real Listeners

Set up **free helplines** in every regional language, answered by kind, trained humans not machines.

Why? Because sometimes, all a person needs, is to be heard with kindness.

3. Free Legal Aid for Debt Cases

Most farmers do not understand legal rights. Free lawyers and student volunteers can help them negotiate fairly with lenders and avoid exploitation.

Why? Because fear of debt often leads to suicide. Solutions to the Debt burden in Door 2, Remember?

4. Pesticide Regulation

Make sure pesticides the most common suicide tool are sold only with ID and under supervision.

Why? Reduce access during crisis = reduce suicide attempts.

5. Crop Insurance That Actually Pays on Time

Use technology like drones and satellite data to assess crop loss quickly and disburse claims within **15 days.**

Why? Because help delayed is help denied.

6. Emergency Farmer Work Groups

Create village collectives where struggling farmers can earn daily wages by growing quick-yield crops together.

Why? Work brings dignity and community.

7. Adoption Programs for Farmer Families

Urban citizens, NRIs, or companies can "adopt" a farmer family offering monthly support and emotional connection.

Why? Knowing someone cares is powerful medicine.

8. Monthly Farmer Wellness Days

A day each month for relaxation, health checkups, yoga, fun games and community bonding.

Why? We celebrate everything then why not celebrate the people who feed us?

9. Public Honor Boards

Villages should have walls showing photos and names of hardworking farmers. This recognition will encourage them to core.

Why? Honor builds pride and pride protects mental health.

10. Financial Literacy Training

Teach farmers how to budget, use apps, access government schemes and avoid loan traps.

Why? Empowerment through education.

11. School Programs for Farming Families' Children

Let children grow up with pride in their farmer parents not shame.

Why? Educated kids protect their families better.

12. National Campaign to Rebrand Farming

Use media, movies, books and influencers to show farming as a **noble, skilled and dignified profession.**

Why? Respect changes mindset. Mindset saves lives.

I don't sleep much," a farmer once told a researcher.
"I just stare at the roof and worry. But I can't tell anyone. What will they say?"

That line pierced my heart.

How can we eat in peace, when the one who grows our food sleeps in worry? How can our meals nourish us,

When the hands that sowed it were trembling with anxiety...

When the heart that nurtured the crop was aching in silence?

I was raised with a sacred teaching from my elders: **Food made or served in sorrow can never become health.**

If someone cooks for you while crying, or serves you while feeling broken,

or grows your grains with a burdened soul,

then that food, no matter how rich, carries unseen pain.

And that's why...

I dream of a Bharat where no farmer feels unloved or unheard.

Where every grain is grown not just with effort, but with dignity and joy.

Because only then can we call our meals complete. Only then can we say with pride:

"This food not only fills my stomach.....it blesses my soul."

Let us not just thank the farmer after harvest.

Let us stand by them before the seeds even touch the soil. Can we do this?

Legal Rights of Farmers in India: Empowering the Hands That Feed the Nation

1. Right to Land & Cultivation

Farmers have the legal right to own, lease, or inherit agricultural land under state-specific land laws.

- Hindu Succession Act (Amendment, 2005): Grants equal rights to daughters in ancestral agricultural land.
- Tenancy Rights: Some states allow tenant farmers to legally claim land they have tilled for years, ensuring security of tenure.

"If a farmer has cultivated land continuously, he may have legal protection as a 'Protected tenant' in states like Andhra Pradesh or Maharashtra."

2. Right to Fair Pricing

Minimum Support Price (MSP) is a government-fixed price at which it buys crops from farmers, ensuring they don't have to sell below cost.

- **Set by the** Commission for Agricultural Costs and Prices (CACP)
- Applicable to 23 major crops like wheat, rice, pulses, etc.
- Legal right to **demand MSP in mandis** (agricultural markets)

Limitation: Not all farmers benefit equally due to lack of procurement in some regions.

3. Right to Market Freedom

APMC Act Reforms: Farmers can now sell their produce:

- In mandis (markets)
- Directly to consumers or businesses
- Online or via mobile apps

Farmers are not legally bound to sell only through state-run mandis anymore (in most states).

4. Right to Insurance & Compensation

Pradhan Mantri Fasal Bima Yojana (PMFBY): A farmer-friendly insurance scheme covering:

- Crop failure due to drought, flood, pests, etc.
- Delayed sowing or germination failure
- Post-harvest losses

Legal right to compensation if enrolled and eligible.

"If a farmer loses crops, he can legally claim insurance within 72 hours of the event through his village-level officer."

5. Right to Credit & Protection from Exploitation

Access to Institutional Credit: Farmers can take loans at subsidized interest from

- NABARD
- Regional Rural Banks
- Co-operative Banks
- Kisan Credit Cards (KCC)

6. Debt Relief & Loan Waivers

While not a constitutional right, **state governments can legally announce waivers** in cases of extreme distress.

7. Protection from Moneylenders

- **Usurious Loans Act:** Prevents charging of excessive interest
- Farmers can file cases of exploitation in local courts or with the district magistrate

8. Right to Government Support Schemes: PM-KISAN

- ₹6,000/year paid directly into the bank accounts of eligible small and marginal farmers.

- Legal right once registered with land records and Aadhaar

9. Right to Information & Transparency RTI Act, 2005

Farmers can file Right to Information requests to:

- Know status of subsidy disbursements
- Get updates on land acquisition
- Verify whether MSP procurement is happening

10. Grievance Redressal

Farmers can legally file complaints with:

- Agriculture officers
- State Lokayuktas
- Consumer courts (in case of spurious seeds, fake fertilizers)

11. Right to Livelihood & Dignity

Though not always directly enforceable, the Right to Livelihood is a fundamental right under Article 21.

- State has a legal and moral duty to create an environment where farmers can live a life of dignity and financial stability.
- Courts have repeatedly ruled that suicide due to crop failure or debt is a failure of governance.

12. Special Protections for Women Farmers

While laws still need to improve, women farmers have:

- Right to inherit land
- Right to open KCC accounts
- Right to participate in Self-Help Groups (SHGs)
- Legal eligibility for all government schemes

"She is not just a farmer's wife, she is a farmer too."

13. Right to Education for Farmer Children

Under the **Right to Education Act, 2009,** children from farming families are entitled to:

- Free and compulsory education (ages 6-14)
- Special provisions if parent is disabled or deceased
- Reservation under **EWS or SC/ST/OBC** depending on category.

What Can You Do? A Reader's Responsibility:

You may not be a policymaker. You may not be a farmer.

But you are a citizen of this soil and **you can make a difference.**

Here are **real, simple things** you can do to support farmers and contribute to a **Suicide Mukt Bharat**:

1. **Support Local Farmers**
    - Buy directly from **farmers' markets**, mandis and small vendors.
    - Promote and share platforms that connect farmers directly to buyers cutting out exploitative middlemen.
2. **Educate Yourself and Others**
    - Learn about the real issues farmers face: climate unpredictability, debt cycles, poor irrigation, lack of crop insurance.
    - Talk to your kids, friends and community about *respecting the annadata.*
3. **Break the Silence Around Mental Health**
    - Encourage open discussions about depression and anxiety among farmers.
    - Share mental health quotes to keep openness in your village groups and communities.

4. **Volunteer or Donate**
   - Join NGOs that work on rural mental health, organic farming or farmer education.
   - Donate to verified organizations that help with debt relief or
   - children's education of suicide-affected families.
5. **Be Human, First**
   - If you meet a farmer whether in a field, at a mandi, or in your village look them in the eyes and thank them.
   - **Never treat them as "just a farmer."** They are the ones who keep us alive.

Mythological Insight: When the Gods Touched the Soil:

In our rich Indian mythology, even gods knew the value of farming.

Lord Balarama, the elder brother of Shri Krishna, didn't carry a sword he carried a plough.

Yes, a *hal*, the same tool our farmers use.

He was called *Haladhari* the one who works with the soil. Because farming was never seen as low or ordinary.

It was divine. It was respected.

And when King **Janak** found **Maa Sita** while ploughing the field during a sacred ritual as a baby girl, it was a message for all time:

"The land gives life. The farmer is the giver."

But today, those real-life givers... are dying.

Not because they are weak, but because they feel forgotten. Because we stopped seeing them as divine.

We worship the land on Diwali, on Pongal and on Makar Sankranti...

But we forgot the hands that make it sacred every single day. Remember....

If Lord Balarama could proudly hold a plough,

then we must proudly hold the hand of every farmer who still does.

Indian mythology is **not fiction** it is **spiritual psychology**, wrapped in sacred symbolism. Every tale offers not just entertainment, but emotional guidance.

Closing the Door: But Opening a New Chapter

The pain of our farmers is not just rural pain. It is national pain. When the soil cries, the soul of Bharat cracks.

As you step out of this door, carry this truth in your heart:

Every grain of rice you eat was touched by a man who fought the sun, the soil and sometimes even his own sorrow just to feed you.

Let's not allow him to fight alone anymore. Let this door become your turning point.

- Let your empathy turn into action.
- Let your awareness turn into advocacy.
- Let your voice rise for those whose voices were buried too soon.

And above all ......let's build a **Suicide Mukt Bharat** not just with words, but with will.

Because a country that saves its farmers is a country that saves its future.

LETS BEGIN WITH THE STEPS:

I know you've been through so much already...emotionally, mentally even physically.

But healing doesn't happen all at once. It happens step by step.

And each small step you take from here can lead you closer to peace and back to life.

These steps are not rules. They are lifelines.

Let's walk through them....together, gently one moment at a time."

Before It's Too Late" ..Understanding the Warning Signs
Every reader must learn to ***recognize & rescue*** *someone in crisis.*

STEP ONE:
WARNING SIGNS

1. **Emotional Warning Signs**
   - Saying things like "I don't want to live anymore" or "It would be better if I disappeared."
   - Expressing deep hopelessness or helplessness.
   - Sudden mood swings..calmness after intense depression.
   - Talking about being a burden to others.
2. **Behavioral Changes**
   - Withdrawing from friends, family and activities.
   - Sleeping too much or too little
   - Sudden interest in weapons, pills or online suicide methods.
   - Declining work or academic performance.
   - Increased use of alcohol or drugs.

3. **Mental Health Indicators**

   - Long-term depression or anxiety.
   - Talking about feeling trapped or in unbearable pain.
   - Hallucinations, paranoia or erratic behavior.
   - History of trauma, abuse or previous suicide attempts.

4. **Subtle Signs We Often Ignore**

   - Constantly saying "I'm tired" not just physically, but emotionally.
   - Laughing too much or acting overly normal (forced mask).
   - Cancelling plans often.
   - Talking a lot about death, poems or stories related to loss.
   - Excessive guilt over small things.

STEP TWO:

What You Can Do – Be the Reason Someone Chooses to Stay:

- Don't say "It's just in your head." Say, "I'm here. You're not alone."
- Remove means (sharp objects, pills, ropes) if you suspect risk.
- Don't judge, don't give advice. Just be present.
- Encourage them to talk to a professional and offer to go with them if needed.
- Follow up. Don't just check once and forget. Show up again and again.

STEP THREE:

The Role of Families: Home Can Be a Lifeline or a Lonely Cage

"You live in a house full of people... and still feel unseen. That's when the real suffering begins."

Families can save lives. But they can also unknowingly **crush souls** when they stop listening, judging too quickly, or becoming too busy to notice.

Here's what families must understand & practice:

1. **Learn to Observe, Not Just See**
    - Notice changes in appetite, sleep or social behavior.
    - Don't dismiss sadness as drama or stubbornness.
    - If your child, spouse, sibling, or parent becomes unusually quiet or aggressive pause and ask gently, "What's going on in your heart?"
2. **Create a Non-Judgmental Space**
    - **Avoid phrases like:**
        - "Sab thik ho jaega" (It's all going to be okay)
        - "Itna bhi kya ho gaya?" (Come on, what happened that's so serious?)
        - "Tum weak ho gaye ho" (You've become weak)
    - **Instead, say:**
        - "I'm listening"
        - "You matter to me"
        - "We'll face this together"

Even one safe person in a family can prevent a suicide.

3. **Handle the Storm with Patience** Sometimes, your loved one will push you away. Sometimes they won't talk.

    Sometimes they'll say hurtful things out of pain.

Don't take it personally. Take it patiently.

Their silence is not rejection...it's a cry for safety.

4. **Educate Yourself as a Family**

- Learn about depression, anxiety, schizophrenia and stress- related disorders.
- **Learn the** difference between tantrums and breakdowns.
- If your child says, "I hate myself," don't get angry. Get curious. Ask: *"Why do you feel this way?"*

  Not: *"Don't talk like that!"*

5. **Be the Armor, Not the Arrow**

- Don't shame them in front of others. Ever.
- Don't use mental illness or weakness as a taunt.
- Celebrate their efforts, not just achievements.
- Protect their dignity like you would protect your own.

6. **Talk, Talk, Talk:**

   Make open conversation normal in your house:

- "How was your day..*emotionally?*"
- "Anything troubling your mind lately?"
- "What made you happy this week?"
- "Do you want to cry or vent today?"

These simple questions build lifelong safety.

7. **Take Their Words Seriously**

   If someone says:

- "I feel like dying."
- "I can't take this anymore."

- "I'm a burden."

Never ignore. Never delay. Never laugh it off.

Even if it sounds dramatic it's real to them.

Get help immediately. Even one moment of delay can cost a life.

A Family Can Be the Reason Someone Chooses to Live

A mother's hug, a father's kind word, a sibling's shoulder, a spouse's

Patience. These are not small things. **They are medicine. They are hope.** You don't need perfect answers.

You just need to show up, again and again, until the storm passes.

STEP FOUR:
The Role of Schools, Colleges & Universities:

Where Futures Are Made or Broken

"A child spends more time in classrooms than at home. If the classroom isn't safe for the heart, how will it ever nourish the mind?"

Educational institutions are meant to be temples of learning. But for many students, they become **pressure chambers** where comparison, fear of failure, bullying and silence become unbearable burdens.

To prevent suicides among students, **our schools and colleges must shift from performance-based environments to compassion-based ecosystems.**

1. **Mental Health Education Shouldn't Be Optional**
   - Include **basic emotional literacy** from primary classes onward:
     - "What is stress?"
     - "How do I deal with anxiety?"
     - "Who can I talk to when I feel low?"

- Mental health must be part of the curriculum, not just awareness weeks.

2. **On-Campus Counsellors Must Be Mandatory**
   - Every school and college should have at least one full-time mental health professional.
   - Students should be allowed to access counsellors confidentially, without being judged or reported to parents unless necessary.

3. **Teachers Need Empathy Training**
   - Train teachers to spot early signs of distress: absenteeism, withdrawal, emotional outbursts, sudden academic drop.
   - Teach them to speak with **kindness over criticism.**
   - Even a single sentence like "You matter" from a teacher can stop a child from taking a step toward death.

4. **Bullying Should Be Treated as a Life-Threatening Issue**
   - Schools and universities must have **zero-tolerance policies** toward bullying especially emotional or social exclusion.
   - Anonymous complaint systems should exist.
   - Workshops for students on empathy, kindness and inclusive behavior must be held monthly, not annually.

5. **Stop Treating Grades as a Person's Worth**
   - Educational institutes should evaluate effort, creativity participation--not just marks.
   - Host "*failure conversations*" where students and alumni share how failures shaped their journeys.
   - Celebrate progress, not just perfection.

6. **Create Safe Clubs and Circles**
   - Support groups, talk circles, mental health clubs should be student- led and faculty-supported.

- Monthly "Open Mic for the Soul" sessions where students can share anonymously or publicly about their struggles, fears and hopes.

7. **Build an Environment of Belonging**
    - Address students by name. Smile at them. Make time for them.
    - Recognize lonely students and involve them gently.
    - Remind them: **"Your presence matters here."**

A Campus Can Be a Clinic for the Soul

Imagine an India where no student cries alone in a hostel room... Where no teenager writes a suicide note before an exam... Where teachers, friends and the system say: "You are bigger than your marks. You are loved. You are not alone."

This is not a dream. It is a **necessity.**

And it starts with one school. One teacher.

One principal.

One reader... **like you...** who dares to care.

STEP FIVE:
The Role of Organisations: Corporates & Management
Workplaces That Heal or Harm

"They delivered every deadline. Smiled in every meeting.
But nobody saw the tears in their eyes when the laptop shut down."

In the hustle for profit, human pain becomes invisible.

In the culture of performance, mental collapse is mistaken for laziness.

Today, burnout, chronic stress and silent emotional breakdowns are leading causes of suicide among working professionals especially in India's demanding and competitive work culture.

It's time we ask:

What kind of workplace are we creating?

One that builds lives or breaks them?

1. **Make Mental Health a Management Priority**
    - Mental health isn't a luxury... it's a core responsibility.
    - Appoint **Mental Wellness Officers** in every company even no matter the company has less employees. **Every Employee Matters**
    - Provide **anonymous therapy options** through EAPs (Employee Assistance Programs).
    - Regular mental health surveys to check stress levels and identify red zones.
2. **Redesign Toxic Work Cultures**
    - Say NO to:
        - Overwork glorification
        - 24x7 WhatsApp messages
        - Humiliation during meetings
        - Public scolding or bullying by seniors
    - Say YES to:
        - Work-life balance policies
        - Compassionate leadership
        - Flexible work hours for caregivers or chronically ill employees
3. **Train Managers to Be Emotionally Intelligent**
    - Conduct workshops on:
        - How to talk to an emotionally distressed employee
        - Recognizing signs of burnout or suicidal thoughts

    - Compassionate conflict resolution
- Encourage managers to **ask with heart**, not just targets.

"A manager can be the reason someone holds on or the reason someone let's go."

4. **Create Healing Spaces within the Office**
    - Meditation zones, quiet rooms, in-house counselors, peer support circles.
    - Monthly emotional check-ins, not just project reviews.
    - Organize sessions with **mental health speakers, survivors and experts.**
5. **Policy for Protection**
    - Add clear clauses in the HR manual:
        - Anti-harassment policies (including emotional & mental abuse)
        - Leave support for mental health breakdowns
        - Suicide prevention and postvention protocols
6. **Celebrate Human Effort, Not Just Performance**
    - Acknowledge employees who show emotional growth, courage or honesty.
    - Reward consistency... teamwork, not just sales and output. Because not all achievements are visible on spreadsheets.

Organizations Can Save Lives:

When a workplace values people more than profit, it becomes purpose-driven.
When leadership speaks with kindness, it becomes powerful.
When employees feel safe enough to say "I'm not okay," then true success begins.

We don't just work to earn.

We work to feel valued and respected

Let's build workplaces where suicide never becomes an option because support is always available and dignity is never lost.

STEP SIX:
Healing & Recovery After a Suicide Attempt

"I didn't want to die. I just didn't know how to live with that pain anymore."

The Breath After the Storm

There comes a moment silent, trembling and cold when you open your eyes after trying to leave the world.

The world looks the same... but **you don't.**

Your body is breathing but your soul feels shattered. You hear whispers outside your hospital room "Why did they do it?" You see your mother's red eyes. Your friend's awkward silence. The nurse's kind touch that you can't accept.

And inside you... A question that weighs like a stone in the throat:

"What now?"

The Truth No One Talks About

No one prepares you for the life after a suicide attempt.

No one tells you how it feels to sit in your room, staring at the ceiling.

No one tells you how much courage it takes to pick up your phone and reply to someone who saw your pain too late.

No one talks about the silence, the guilt, the voice inside your head that keeps saying:

"You shouldn't be here..."

But listen......

You should & You Must

Not because everything will suddenly become perfect. But because **You Matter**. Even now. Especially now.

The Invisible Wounds

- You cry in the shower, where no one can hear.
- You smile at your parents so they don't worry again.
- You wake up feeling lost, wondering why you were saved. But I need to tell you something with all my heart:

You are not a mistake. You are a miracle.

You are here not to suffer endlessly, but to slowly, gently, painfully... **HEAL.**

Minor Steps Towards Gentle Healing:

1. Let Yourself Be Helped

Please don't carry it all alone.

Let someone hold your hand. Let a therapist listen. Let your wounds be seen not judged.

2. Let Your Body Recover

It tried to carry too much. Let it rest now.

Drink water. Eat something. Touch your face and whisper: *"You're still here and I love you."*

3. Make a Safety Plan, not a Cage

Write down five reasons to stay. Even if one is as small as "my dog's tail wags when I come home."

Write names of people who make you feel human again. Place it where your pain cannot ignore it

The Mind Will Lie to You

It will say:

- "You are a burden."
- "No one would care if you were gone."
- "You'll never be okay again."

These are lies. Cruel ones.

Don't argue with them. Just breathe through them.

Try to Command Your Brain

And remember..... storms never stay.

But the roots they water inside you? They grow into forests of strength.

Rebuilding Your Soul

Start small:

- Take a walk, barefoot on the grass.
- Write a letter to your younger self.
- Hold someone's hand and let the tears come.
- Plant something. A seed. A hope. Yourself. Healing doesn't ask you to forget the pain.

It asks you to believe that **you are not the pain.**

Mythological Insight for the Survivors:

❖ **Prahlad's Unbreakable Light**

There was a little boy named **Prahlad**, who stood against a world that wanted to destroy him.

He was thrown into fire...

Crushed beneath elephants...

Poisoned by those who should have protected him...

But he didn't fight back with weapons.

He didn't scream or curse his fate.

He simply closed his eyes and held onto one thing the world couldn't take from him. **Faith.**

Faith that no matter how cruel the world became, the divine within him would never abandon him.

Faith that his truth and his innocence... was stronger than any darkness around him.

And that faith saved him not from pain, but **through pain.**

Dear Reader, maybe your fire didn't look like Prahlad's...

Maybe it came in the form of betrayal, loss, illness, loneliness or heartbreak.

Maybe you were crushed not by elephants but by words...

By silence.

By people who saw you're suffering and still walked away. But if you're reading this now, it means one thing:

Your soul didn't give up.

Just like Prahlad, your body may have trembled, your heart may have shattered, but something inside you stayed alive a flicker or a stubborn hope.

Like Prahlad, you don't need the world to believe in you. You need to believe in yourself.

And when you do; truly do- no fire can burn you, no poison can break you and no voice can silence the spiritual strength inside you.

You are not just a survivor.

You are a living miracle.

Closing Reflection

These Doors Were Never Locked...
You Just Needed to Believe You Could Walk Through It...

Dear Reader,

If you've made it this far reading with a lump in your throat, tears you didn't expect or silent nods of recognition then this part is just for you.

You didn't just read a chapter.

You walked through fire with me.

You entered a world where pain is silent, suffering is invisible and strength is misunderstood.

You opened a door that most people pretend doesn't even exist.

But you saw it. You stood before it.

And now, slowly, you're learning to walk through it.

Not with perfect steps.

But with trembling courage.That courage is what will save you

I want you to know something very clearly:

You are not weak because you've suffered. You are strong because you stayed.

Through the diagnosis, the pain, the judgment, the comparisons, the sleepless nights, the shame, the helpless moments where you whispered to God or the ceiling "Why me?"

Through all of it, you remained.

This door isn't about curing illness or removing disability.

It's about one thing helping you remember who you are beyond your pain.

Like the seed that breaks open to bloom.

Like Prahlad, whose suffering didn't destroy him… it awakened him. You too are awakening.

So, keep on leaving those doors you entered.

Walk out with pride. With grace. With purpose.

Let the world look at you and wonder,

"Was this their rebirth?"

Because yes. It was.

And if anyone dares to shame you, doubt you or pity you…

Smile in Front of Them.

And remember Lord Krishna who laughed at every insult and turned every scar into a scripture.

You don't need to prove anything anymore.

You've already lived through what many wouldn't survive.

Now go… not to hide, but to shine. Not to shrink, but to speak.

Because those doors were built to make you feel free.

And your freedom will become someone else's hope.

Keep walking.

I'm with you.

Archana Sinha Bhandari

(A mother, a survivor and a soul who chose to stay.)

A Real Tribute to Real Survivors

To those who didn't give up. Even when everything told them to. This is for every soul who stayed.

For the woman who wiped her tears and still packed lunch. For the man who faced shame.... still walked with dignity. For the student who failed but chose not to fall.

For the person who survived an attempt and now helps others survive too.

You may not have medals or headlines,

but you carry something far more powerful...**a will to live.**

This book is not about their stories.

It's about the **people who lived through it**.

If you're reading this and breathing despite everything

You are the reason this movement exists.

Thank you for surviving. Thank you for staying. The world needs your light.

Archana Sinha Bhandari (ANNA)

In Suicide Mukt Bharat: The Road Ahead

A Final Promise from One Heart to Another

This is not just the closing of a book. This is the opening of a revolution.

A revolution that began with one teardrop.
One sleepless night.
One mother whispering to herself
"I will not let another child feel unloved in this world."

The Cry We've All Ignored Too Long

Behind every suicide is not just a death.
It is a death of trust. A death of hope.
A death that could've been prevented
If only someone had paused and said: "I'm here. You matter."

Let This Be Our Beginning

Let this be the moment where we stop asking: "Why didn't they speak up?"
And start asking: "Were we listening at all?"
Let us become the arms that hold instead of blame.
The voice that comforts instead of questions.

This book is stitched with my tears, yes.

But it is not just mine.
This has to be everyone's mission now....

It belongs to every father who wears a brave face for his family.
To every student crying quietly in the washroom.
To every mother pretending to be strong.

To every child who thinks no one would miss them if they disappeared.

To every soul that ever whispered, "I can't do this anymore."

You can.
We are here to walk with you.

•

One Last Request from the Heart

This is no longer just my journey... It's now yours too.
If this book has touched even a corner of your heart

If any line reminded you of someone you lost...
or someone you could still save
Then please, I ask you:

Don't let it end here.

Support the Suicide Mukt Bharat Movement

Support it in any way you can. Not just with your money

but with your words, your time, your attention, your humanity.

- If you are a parent: be the safe space your child never fears.
- If you are a teacher: be the hand that lifts, not the voice that shames.
- If you are a manager: lead not just with goals, but with grace.
- If you are a friend: check on the one who laughs the loudest.
- If you are just you: be kind. Be present. Be real.

You Don't Have to Start a Movement.
Just be the movement.

In your home. In your WhatsApp groups. In your words. In your silence.

Share this book. Gift it to someone.

Talk about suicide prevention even if it feels uncomfortable.

Join hands with NGOs. Support therapy access.

Raise your voice against bullying, injustice and apathy.

Be the reason someone believes:

"I matter."

Because I Can't Do This Alone...

But together, we can build a nation that breathes with empathy.

Where suicide is not a secret anymore.

Where every soul, no matter how wounded, finds hope, help and healing.

So today, I ask you

From one human to another

Will you walk with me?

Will you support Suicide Mukt Bharat in every little way you can?

For someone you love. For someone you lost.
For someone you haven't met yet...
But whose life your love might save.

With folded hands, With a hopeful heart,
And with unshakable faith in you,

Archana Sinha Bhandari
Founder, Voice and Soul of the Suicide Mukt Bharat Movement

A Mother. A *Survivor*. A Witness to the Pain. A Light for the Healing.